Sylt
57
63 54
10
Kiel
51
Rügen
65
40
66
49
Rostock
Usedom
33 38
Hamburg
44 47
1
60
53
Berlin
48
Hannover
2
12
18
6 39
45
26
21
15 59
35
25 24
Leipzig
41
Köln
20
Dresden
9
4
8
7
23 34
Frankfurt
28 16
37
42
32
13 58
Nürnberg
52
61 50
46
11
55
14 43 64
Stuttgart
29 5
22
67 36
3
19
17
München
31
27 30
56
62

Fast vorbeigefahren: Club für Paare
Almost unnoticed: Club for Couples

Übersehene Sehenswürdigkeiten. Deutsche Orte.

Overlooked Sights. German Places.

Michaela Vieser und Reto Wettach

ic! berlin

Die Autoren danken folgenden Personen für ihre Hilfe:

Baldur, Björn Andresen, Carolin Hauber, Christian Humborg, Heidi & Geert, Helga & Theo, Jack Kerouac, Jan Brandt, Lucinda Newton-Dunn, Mirja Li und Ralph Anderl, Nathan Moore, Susanne Lüdtke, Tsuzuki Kyoichi, Ulrich Oettinger, Veronika Schallnau und allen in diesem Werk gennanten Orten und den Menschen, die uns dort betreut haben.

Außerdem folgenden Firmen für ihre großzügige Unterstützung:

Apple Japan, e-plus, ic! berlin, papersky, Sony Europe, Volkswagen

Abdruck Karte Seite 1 mit freundlicher Genehmigung des Bundesamts für Kartographie und Geodäsie, Frankfurt a. M.
Abdruck Karte Seite 155 mit freundlicher Genehmigung des Klosters Ebstorf

Die Deutsche Bibliothek – CIP-Einheitsaufnahme:

Vieser, Michaela; Wettach, Reto:
Übersehene Sehenswürdigkeiten. Deutsche Orte. Overlooked Sights. German Places.
ic! berlin, Berlin
2. Auflage 2005
ISBN 3-9809758-0-0

Saarbrücker Str. 37
10405 Berlin / Germany
www.ic-berlin.de
book@ic-berlin.de

Autoren: friends@driftingfriends.de, www.driftingfriends.de

Umschlaggestaltung: Lucinda Newton-Dunn
Satz: Björn Andresen
Übersetzung: Nathan Moore

Druck und Bindung: Jütte-Messedruck Leipzig GmbH

Serendipity – The Art of Drifting

Serendipity – The Art of Drifting

Serendipity ist ein englisches Kunstwort, das der Briefeschreiber Horace Walpole (1754) erfunden hat. Es beschreibt die Kunst und das Vergnügen, etwas zu finden, das man nicht gesucht hat. Oder, wie es Julius H. Comroe, ein biomedizinischer Forscher ausdrückte:
„Serendipity bedeutet nach der Nadel im Heuhaufen zu suchen und statt dessen die Tochter des Bauerns zu finden."
Sechs Monate lang waren wir im VW-Bus unterwegs in Deutschland, auf der Suche nach „übersehenen Sehenswürdigkeiten". Wir suchten die unbekannten oder vergessenen Orte. Orte fernab von den 08/15 Reiseführertipps, Orte mit Geschichten, die es wert sind, erzählt zu werden. Unsere Vorab-Recherche war weder im Internet noch in der Literatur erfolgreich: Die Orte, die wir suchten, konnten nur unterwegs entdeckt werden. Wir aßen in Landgasthöfen, besuchten lokale Architekten, hakten nach. Immer mit derselben Frage: „Gibt es hier einen besonderen Ort, den man nur hier kennt?" Wenn wir so einen Ort gefunden hatten, konnten wir ihn bei der weiteren Suche als Beispiel angeben. Das half. So führte uns eine übersehene Sehenswürdigkeit zur nächsten. Die 67 besten sind hier in diesem Buch zusammengefasst. Viel Spaß beim Entdecken.

Michaela Vieser und Reto Wettach

Serendipity is a made up word that was invented by the British letter-writer, Horace Walpole (1754). It describes the art and joy of discovering something which you had not set out to find. Or, as Biomedical Researcher Julius H. Comroe put it:
"Serendipity is looking for a needle in a haystack and finding the Farmer's Daughter."
On the road in Germany for six months in a VW-Bus, in search of "overlooked sights," we were hunting for unknown or forgotten places, far from the beaten old travel-guide path – places with stories worth telling. Our preparatory research could not be done on the internet or taken from books: The places which we were searching for could only be found on the road. We ate at country-side inns, visited local architects, and nosed around persistently, always with the same question: "Is there a some kind of special place around here… a place that only people from around here know about?" After finding such places, we were then able to use them as examples on our quest for the next. That helped. In this way, one overlooked sight led to another. The best 67 of these are collected here in this book. Have a great time discovering.

Michaela Vieser and Reto Wettach

Vorwort
Preface

Entscheidet sich in Japan ein junger Mensch während seiner Universitätszeit für eine neue Sprache, so wählt er meist zwischen der französischen oder der deutschen. Je nachdem welche der beiden Sprachen dieser junge Mensch dann wählt, erlauben wir uns, seinen Charakter einzustufen: gehört er der deutschen Fraktion an, so glauben wir zu wissen, er sei ernsthaft, habe eine konservative Weltanschauung und leide generell unter schlechtem Geschmack.
Wir Japaner stehen den Deutschen im Reisen um nichts nach. Die jungen Japaner gehen gerne nach Rom und Paris, während sich die japanischen Großväterchen und Großmütterchen auf Süddeutschland und den Schwarzwald stürzen.
Fragt man einen Japaner, was er mit Deutschland assoziiert, so fallen bestimmt folgende Begriffe: Mercedes Benz, BMW, Bier, Fußball, klassische Musik, die Romantische Straße und Neuschwanstein.
Ich habe mich oft gefragt, an was die anderen Europäer bei Deutschland denken.

In Japan, when students begin their studies at the university, they will generally choose between two languages: French or German. We like to say that the character of a student is clearly shown in their choice of language. Well, those of the German fraction are considered to be serious minded, of conservative nature, and of unrefined taste.
When it comes to traveling, we Japanese are about as bad as the Germans. Paris and Rome are favorites among young Japanese, whereas Japan's Grandpas and Grandmas prefer places in Southern Germany and the Black Forest. If a Japanese person is asked what his idea of Germany is, he will most likely answer: Mercedes Benz, BMW, beer, soccer, classical music, the Romantic Road and Neuschwanstein. I often wonder what kind of image other Europeans have of Germany.
I always enjoyed looking for places to put into my "Roadside Europe" book. As I live in Japan, it was always necessary to prepare myself ahead of time, researching places before actually visiting them. Whenever I was getting ready for a

Es hat mir immer großen Spaß gemacht, nach Orten für mein „Roadside Europe" Buch zu suchen. Meine Recherche nach Orten dort begann immer zu Hause in Japan, vor meiner eigentlichen Reise. So habe ich also meine Reisebücher konsultiert, schaute auf Websites nach oder begnügte mich mit der allgemein zugänglichen Information eines Landes. Es war aber immer Deutschland, das am wenigsten zugänglich war. Natürlich fand ich überall mehr als genug Einträge über das Land und seine normalen touristisch

trip, whether I looked in guidebooks, at websites, or just for general information about a country, I found that, as a matter of fact, the hardest country to get information on was Germany. Of course, there were more than enough listings, with all of the usual places, but finding a spot that was even a small step removed, away from the mainstream, was impossible. While there are already lots of books written on strange people and places in England or France, I could find nothing on Germany.

erschlossenen Gebiete, aber einen Ort zu finden, der nur ein klein wenig jenseits der Touristenattraktionen liegt, war mir unmöglich. Obwohl es viele Bücher über seltsame Orte und Menschen in England oder Frankreich gibt, fand ich nichts dergleichen für Deutschland.

Egal welche Grundwerte eine Gesellschaft hat, es wird immer ein Interesse an den Menschen, die „anders" sind, geben. Die Engländer lieben zum Beispiel exzentrische Menschen, auch wenn dieser Charakterzug nur minimal ausgeprägt sein sollte. Ein Engländer denkt sich: „Bin nicht auch ich selbst ein wenig exzentrisch?"

Bei den Franzosen ist diese Liebe für das „Andersgeartete" nicht weniger populär. Nur ist der Hintergedanke hier: „Wenn ich mich mit dieser exzentrischen Person vergleiche, finde ich mich zum Glück ziemlich normal."

Auch in Deutschland gibt es viele Menschen, die kein Leben nach Norm leben. Sollte es daher nicht auch ein großes Interesse von Seiten der anderen Europäer, aber auch der Deutschen selbst geben, diese Kultur zu entdecken?

Bisher habe ich nie eine Antwort auf diese Frage erhalten, aber ich denke, dass dieses Buch ein Schlüssel zu diesem Rätsel ist.

Tsuzuki Kyoichi, August 2004

No matter what kind of values a society has, there will always be an interest in places or people that are different. The English, for example, love people for their eccentricities, however slight these may be. An English person thinks: "After all, I am somewhat eccentric." In France this love for "eccentrics" can be found to no lesser degree. The difference is that there, the thought behind it is: "Compared to all these weirdos, I actually seem to be quite normal." Germany is also full of people who choose to live eccentric lives. Should there not be a keen interest on the part of Europeans, as well as the Germans themselves, to find out about this culture? I have not yet been able to figure out why this does not seem to be the case, but I am happy that this book will be a key in solving this riddle.

Tsuzuki Kyoichi, August 2004

Einmannwelten

One-Man Worlds

Das Lügenmuseum
The Museum of Lies

Der Legende nach entstand das Lügenmuseum der damals 11-jährigen Emma von Hohenbüssow 1884 im Schloss Gantikow. Emma wollte keine Puppenstube wie andere Gleichaltrige, sondern ein Museum. Da sie an diesem Wunsch festhielt, suchten die Eltern alles Kuriose auf dem Dachboden zusammen und legten es im Pavillon aus. Als der Zweite Weltkrieg ausbrach, wurden alle Gegenstände fein säuberlich beschriftet, in Kisten gepackt und auf dem Speicher verstaut. Vieles wurde von Flüchtlingen geplündert, einiges landete 1980 auf einer Müllkippe. Durch Zufall fand ein wandernder Künstler die Exponate mitsamt einem Büchlein über die Geschichte des Lügenmuseums und baute das Museum wieder auf.
Das ist alles Lüge.
Was einen wirklich in Gantikow erwartet, ist weit fantastischer: „Die Lüge im Dienste der Wahrheit wäscht den Staub des Alltags von den Sternen". Unter diesem Leitspruch sind hier 1001 Objekte in neun Räumen durch Licht-, Klang- und Duftinstallationen in Szene gesetzt. Man kann hier zum Beispiel das abgeschnittene Ohr von Vincent van Gogh bewundern. Richtig laut sind die unzähligen Knattermaschinen. Es gibt aber auch subtile Töne wie die Tonbandmitschnitte von den letzten Momenten der unterge-

The museum of lies was established in the castle of Gantikow in 1884. Its founder, the 11-year old Emma von Hohenbüssow, had become tired of taking care of her ordinary old dolls and asked her parents to give her a museum to look after. The obliging parents collected all sorts of objects, put them together into a pavilion, and declared the collection to be Emma's very own "Museum of Lies."
At the start of WWII, all of the museum's objects were labeled, packed into boxes and hidden away in the attic. Large parts of the collection were later ransacked, and the remains were then disposed of at a garbage dump. In the 80's, the wandering artist Richard von Gigantikow stumbled upon the remains of the Museum of Lies purely by coincidence. Fascinated by the idea, he started to rebuild the museum.
This is all a lie.
What is really shown in Gantikow, however, is even more fantastic: "The lie in service of the truth wipes the dust of the ordinary from the stars." Based on this maxim, the museum displays 1001 objects in 9 different rooms, all tied together by light, sound and scent. As you stroll through the corridors of the strange collection, you can listen to the last sounds of the Titanic, see Vincent Van Gogh's ear, or sit on

Das Lügenmuseum von außen
Exterior of the Museum of Lies

henden Titanic. In einem Zimmer schwebt ein fliegender Teppich, ein anderes ist ganz der „Psychodelika Maschinka" gewidmet, die angeblich den Fall der Mauer ausgelöst haben soll. Gleich daneben befindet sich das Geburtszimmer von Willy Brandt. Man kann auch ein kosmisches Wunder bestaunen oder das Vittoriale der Ostdeutschen betreten, das vollgestopft ist mit Souvenirs aus der ehemaligen DDR. Eines ist sicher: aus dem Staunen kommt man so schnell nicht heraus.

a flying carpet. One entire room has been dedicated to the "Psychodelika Maschinka," which – according to the guide – was responsible for the fall of the Berlin Wall in 1989. In the neighboring room, you will find the birthplace of Willy Brandt, one of Germany's most famous Social Democrats. The East German display case is stuffed full with all sorts of souvenirs from the former GDR and bathed in red light. Even a cosmic wonder of the world is shown in one part of the museum. Impossible you say? Nothing is impossible in a museum of lies.

Die Psychodelika Maschinka
The Psychodelika Maschinka

Das Vittoriale der Ostdeutschen
The East German Vittoriale

Das Lügenmuseum
The Museum of Lies
Am Anger 1
16866 Kyritz-Gantikow

p: 033971. 54782

f: 033971. 30084

e: info@luegenmuseum.de

www.luegenmuseum.de

Öffnungszeiten:
täglich
10.00 – 18.00 Uhr

Opening hours:
every day
10 am – 6 pm

Geschnitzter Lebenstraum

A Life of Carving

„Wenn ich erst mal 80 Jahre tot bin, werden die Menschen endlich wissen, was für ein großartiger Künstler ich war", sprach der 1912 verstorbene Eigenbrödler Karl Junker zu den Bürgern von Lemgo. In den 20er Jahren wurde er zumindest in dem Buch „Bildnerei der Geisteskranken" als Beispiel schizophrener Kunst erwähnt und in den 50er Jahren berichtete die Münchner Illustrierte über sein „Geisterhaus".

Das so genannte Geisterhaus ist allerdings gar nicht als solches zu verstehen. Junker, der als Waise aufgewachsen war, sehnte sich nach Liebe und Geborgenheit. Nachdem er sein Kunststudium an der Akademie in München beendet hatte, baute er für sich und die Liebe seines Lebens 1889 in Lemgo ein zweistöckiges Fachwerkhaus. Da die Liebe nie erschien, verbrachte er fast 20 Jahre mit der Gestaltung des Hauses: Er beschnitzte alles, sowohl die Fassade, als auch das Innere. Kein Quadratzentimeter blieb unbeschnitzt. Selbst die Toilette ist mit Filigranschnitzereien übersät. Und kleine Zwischenräume bemalte er mit anthroposophisch anmutenden Bildern, die er seinen Träumen entnahm: Urmütter, Phalli und glückliche Menschen. Die Leute aus Lemgo fanden das alles zu sonderbar und machten einen großen Bogen um Junkers Haus. Obwohl es nach seinem Tode zum Verkauf stand, wollte nie mehr jemand einziehen. Jetzt sind die 80 Jahre vergangen, und tatsächlich kümmert sich nun die NRW-Stiftung um die Erhaltung des Junker-Hauses. Inzwischen wird er nicht mehr als schizophrener Künstler, sondern als Vertreter der „Art Brut" verstanden.

Karl Junker died in 1912, but he used to tell his neighbors, "Eighty years after my death, people will finally understand that I was a great artist." In the 1920's, after he had passed away, his work was at least mentioned in a book: "Bildnerei der Geisteskranken" ("Art of the Mentally Ill"), as an example of art created by schizophrenics. Later in the 50's, an article on his "Ghost House" was even published in the Münchner Illustrierte.

This so-called Ghost House, however, is not actually haunted. Having grown up as an orphan, Junker had spent his entire life looking for love and security. After completing his studies at the Art Academy in Munich in 1889, he went back to his hometown of Lemgo and started building a two-story half-timbered house which was to house the love of his life. This love, unfortunately, never appeared, and he continued working on the house for the next 20 years.

Every part of the building was hand carved by the artist, exterior as well as interior. Not a single corner remained uncarved. Even the toilet is overflowing with filigree carving. The small remaining spaces between the carvings were then painted with various scenes from the artist's dream life. Fat mother earth like goddesses, huge phalluses and happy families adorn the interior of Junker's world.

The people of Lemgo found this all a bit strange and always tried to avoid the house and its owner. After Junker's death, the building was put up for sale at a very low price, but there were no buyers to be found.

Eighty years have now passed, and just as he predicted, his work is beginning to be noticed by Germany's cultural stratum. The Nordrhein Westphalen Foundation has become involved in conserving the house, and Junker is no longer seen as a schizophrenic artist, but as an important representative of Art Brut.

Das Ehebett von Junker
Junker's matrimonial bed

Filigran geschnitzte Decke
Filigree roof carving

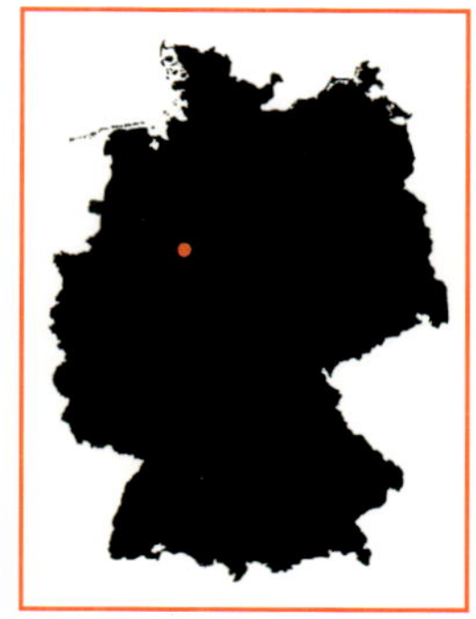

Das Junker-Haus
The Junker-House
Hamelner Straße 36
32657 Lemgo

p: 05261. 213276

www.junkerhaus.de

Öffnungszeiten:
Sonntags
15.00 – 16.30 Uhr
und nach Vereinbarung

Opening hours:
Sundays
3 pm – 4.30 pm
and by arrangement

Das Junker-Haus von außen
Exterior of the Junker House

Märchen in Stein
A Fairy Tale in Stone

Man würde sich ja öfter wünschen, dass reiche Leute sich so richtig spannende Projekte ausdenken. Wenigstens von den Königen hätte man erwarten können, phantastische Schlösser oder Lebenswelten zu verwirklichen. Doch auch die Könige beschränkten sich meist nur darauf, ihre Schlösser nach den zeitgenössischen Regeln der Macht zu bauen. Eine Ausnahme sind die bekannten Schlösser von Bayernkönig Ludwig II. Weniger bekannt dagegen ist das 1840–42 von Graf Wilhelm von Württemberg (übrigens der Onkel des Bayernkönigs) erbaute Schloss Lichtenstein am Rande der Schwäbischen Alb. Nach dem gleichnamigen Märchen „Lichtenstein" von Wilhelm Hauff wurde das Märchenschloss mit herrlich weiß strahlenden Zinnen auf einem Fels thronend errichtet. Der Bayernkönig war hier als Kind oft und gerne zu Besuch – möglicherweise dienten die Erinnerungen daran als Inspirationsquelle für seine Schlösser. Wer den Hof von Lichtenstein betritt, denkt unmittelbar an rauschende Feste, die hier abgehalten wurden – doch belehrt der Schlossführer gleich eines Besseren: Die Württemberger, die hier wohnten, kannten nur „schaffe, schaffe, Häusle baue" und von dekadenten Bällen wollten sie nichts wissen. Schade, denn die Kulisse wäre perfekt gewesen. Hier wurde in zünftiger Runde den bodenständigen Dingen, wie dem Jagen und dem Saufen, gefrönt. Darauf deuten jedenfalls die Trinksprüche in einem der Räume hin. Besonders literarisch ging es dabei allerdings nicht zu: „Es ersaufen viel mehr in Bier und Wein, als in Donau und Rhein" heißt es da, oder „Bisch du krank als wie ein Huhn, magsch nix esse un nix tun." Fürstliche Binsenweisheiten.
Besonders schön zu genießen ist das Schloss an einem lauen Sommerabend im Park mit Picknick, es ist ein Gefühl wie im Märchen. Wer Glück hat trifft dabei auf die alte Gräfin von Urbach, die noch immer hier wohnt, auf ihrem Abendspaziergang.

Wouldn't it be great, if rich people always came up with really exciting things to do with their money? You would think that at least kings might spend their riches achieving the realisation of fantastic dream worlds, filled with majestic castles, full of amazing details. Unfortunately though, most kings were content with a couple of plain old every-day-castles, built to fit in with the norm of the day. There are a few exceptions, however, the most famous of which are King Ludwig II's castles in Bavaria. Less well known is the castle Lichtenstein, built between 1840 and 1842 by Ludwig's uncle, Lord Wilhelm of Württemberg. Based on the fairy tale novel of the same name, Lichtenstein, by Wilhelm Hauff, the castle was erected with shining white pinnacles, high up on a rock. As a child, King Ludwig II had spent many days in this castle, probably taking from it his inspiration for Neuschwanstein.
On entering the castle, you might envision decadent feasts and balls taking place. The guide will dispel this misgiving however. Lord Wilhelm and his family were typical Schwaben (Swabians, as the people of the region are called) and, as a Swabian children's song recites, were interested mainly in "Schaffe, Schaffe, Häusle baue" (work work and build your house). The Lords at castle Lichtenstein tended to enjoy more down to earth entertainment such as hunting and drinking. The walls in the castle bar are covered with rustic drinking sayings, all without literary quality of any kind. Among these are, "More people are drowning in beer and wine than in the rivers of the Mosel or Rhine," or, "If you're as sick as a chicken, you won't be able to eat or work." True aristocratic platitudes.
We recommend visiting the castle on a warm summer's night and having a picnic in the park. You will feel just as if you are in a fairy tale. If you are lucky, you might even meet the old Countess of Urbach on her evening walk. She is still living in the castle.

Das Tor von innen
The castle gate from the inside

Märchenhaftes Haus auf dem Schlossgelände
Fairy-tale like house on the castle grounds

Schloß Lichtenstein
Castle of Lichtenstein
72805 Lichtenstein

p: 07129. 4102

f: 07129. 5259

www.schloss-lichtenstein.de

Öffnungszeiten:
April bis Oktober:
täglich geöffnet
9.00 – 12.00 und
13.00 – 17.30 Uhr
November, Februar, März:
nur Sa, So und an Feiertagen geöffnet
10.00 – 16.00 Uhr

Opening hours:
April to October:
every day
10 am – noon and
1 pm – 5 pm
November, February, March:
only on Weekends
10 am – 4 pm

Das Schloss in seiner ganzen Pracht
The castle in all its majesty

Detailansicht
Detail

Barocke Puppenwelten
Baroque Doll Worlds

Hier handelt es sich um keine Ein-Mann-Welt, sondern um eine Eine-Frau-Welt: Die kinderlose und schnell verwitwete Gräfin Auguste Dorothea von Schwarzenburg-Arnstadt (1666 – 1751) hatte nebst ihren kleinen Hunden ein weiteres niedliches Hobby: Die Nachbildung ihres barocken Umfelds en miniature.
So verbrachte sie die Jahre 1704 – 1751 mit dem Aufbau von „Mon Plaisier – mein Vergnügen", einer Welt aus 82 Puppenstuben und über 400 Puppen. Alles wird hier gezeigt, was sich eine in einem Lustschloss residierende Gräfin unter „Alltagsleben" vorstellt: Bäckerstuben, Gaukler, Nonnen beim Gebet, Kinder beim Spielen, Hausfrauen beim Tratschen. Sogar die Leidensstationen Jesu auf seinem Weg zur Kreuzigung sind mit Puppen nachgestellt. Auffallend viele Szenen von Kaffee trinkenden Damen in angenehmer Runde und höfischem Geplänkel deuten auf den gängigen Zeitvertreib der Gräfin selbst hin.
Jede Szene ist mit echten, eigens dafür angefertigten Porzellanrequisiten bestückt worden. Die Kleider der Puppen sind bis ins letzte Detail ausgeführt.
Es ist dokumentiert, dass sich die Gräfin beim Aufbau ihrer einmaligen Puppenstube hoch verschuldete, vor allem beim nahen Frauenkloster. Darum mußte sie ihre letzten Lebensjahre dort verbringen.
Die Puppenstuben der Gräfin zeigen das barocke Leben nur aus einer Perspektive, nämlich aus der Sicht der herrschenden Klasse. Es handelt sich um eine weltweit einzigartige Sammlung.

This is not a one-man-world, but a one-woman-world. Besides taking care of her cute little dogs, the early widowed and childless Countess Auguste Dorothea von Schwarzenberg-Arnstadt (1666 – 1751) had another cute little hobby as well: the replication of the Baroque world around her into miniature proportions. She spent the years between 1704 and 1751 working on her composition, "Mon Plaisir" ("My Pleasure"), an entire world consisting of 82 dolls' houses and more than 400 dolls. Everything which could possibly have been imagined by a pleasure palace residing Countess has been recreated here: work in the bakery, traveling jugglers, praying nuns, and chatting housewives. Even the painful Stations of the Cross, leading up to Jesus' crucifixion, are recounted here using porcelain dolls. The numerous scenes depicting various ladies enjoying a pleasant cup of tea together point toward the immense amount of free time which the Countess must have had at her disposal, unlike many others of her time.
Each scene was created using uniquely prepared porcelain, and the dolls' clothes were sewn with an intense intricacy. Not a single detail was overlooked.
The costs of her hobby were so outrageously high that she was forced to take out loans, mostly from the nearby monastery. When she got older and was so broke that she was unable to pay back her loans, she decided to move into the monastery, where she lived the life of a nun. While her dolls' houses tend only to reflect the more privileged perspectives of Baroque life, the collection is still interesting in its absolute singularity.

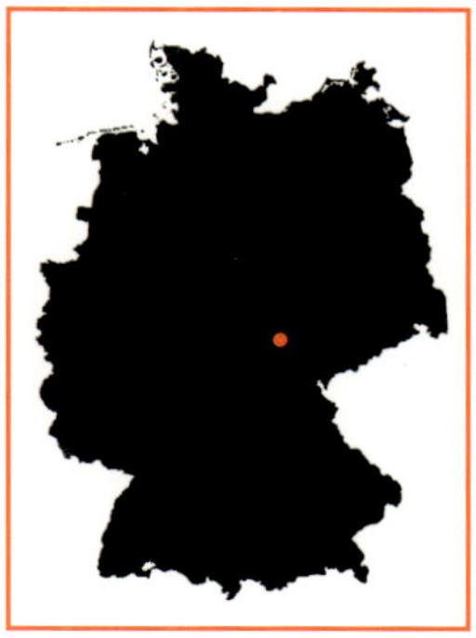

Puppenhäuser und ihr Innenleben: mal Kreuzigung, mal herrschaftliche Rasur
Dolls' houses and there inner workings: here a crucifixion, there a pleasant shave

Puppensammlung „Mon Plaisir“
Doll Collection “Mon Plaisir”
Schlossplatz 1
99310 Arnstadt

p: 03628. 602 932

f: 03628. 482 64

e: schlossmuseum.arnstadt@t-online.de

www.arnstadt.de

Öffnungszeiten:
Im Sommer:
Di bis So
9.30 – 16.30 Uhr
Im Winter:
Di bis So
10.00 – 16.30 Uhr

Opening hours:
In summer:
Tue to Sun
9.30 am – 4.30 pm
In winter:
Tue to Sun
10 am – 4.30 pm

Ein Schlachtfeld in Beton
A Battlefield in Concrete

In einer begrasten Mondlandschaft eröffnet sich dem Wanderer das Figurenfeld Eichstätt. Dichtgedrängt stehen hier 78 überlebensgroße abstrakte Gebilde aus Beton, manche bis zu sechs Tonnen schwer. Da weder ein Schild darauf hinweist, noch ein gefälliger Wandelpfad oder ein Zaun die Kunstinstallation zusammenfassen, könnte man meinen, die Betonklötze seien vom Himmel gepurzelt oder Relikte einer untergegangenen Kultur. Sie sind ein privates Mahnmal gegen Krieg und Gewalt. Keine religiöse oder politische Organisation hat sie in Auftrag gegeben – hier steht das Lebenswerk des Bildhauers Alois Wünsche-Mitterecker. Der aus der Steiermark stammende Künstler verbrachte neun Jahre in Krieg und Gefangenschaft – genug, um ihn für den Rest seines Lebens zu einem mahnenden Figurenfeld zu motivieren. 25 Jahre lang arbeitete Wünsche-Mitterecker an der Umsetzung seiner Vision. Die letzten Figuren wurden erst 1979, vier Jahre nach seinem Tod nach seinen Plänen aufgestellt.
Getrieben von seinen eigenen Erfahrungen hat Alois Wünsche-Mitterecker dieses Projekt nahezu alleine realisiert. Die kleine Broschüre, die bei der Touristeninfo ausliegt, beschreibt diese Anhäufung von Beton als „Schlachtfeld ohne Sieger oder Besiegte". Ob das Ganze nicht doch ein Kultplatz für Außerirdische ist oder zumindest in einigen Jahren so interpretiert werden wird?

Out of a green moon landscape, a small valley littered with stone figures opens up to the roaming traveler. Seventy-eight oversized abstract sculptures made of concrete, weighing up to 6 tons each, are huddled together here. Nature has left its traces on the artwork, and the sculptures meld wonderfully into the roughness of the surrounding valley. There is no well-hewn trail leading to the installation, and it is neither surrounded by a fence nor marked by a sign, giving the impression that the stones have either fallen from the sky or are somehow relics of a perished civilization. In actuality, the sculptures constitute a private memorial against war and terror. Commissioned neither by a religious group or political institution, they represent the life's work of sculptor Alois Wünsche-Mitterecker. The artist was born in the Steiermark, in Austria, and spent 9 years of his life in war and imprisonment. This was enough to motivate him to dedicate the rest of his life to creating this stunning memorial. Working primarily alone, he spent 25 years on the realization of his vision. The last figures were erected in 1979, four years after the artist's death.
In the little booklet that is handed out by the tourist information center, this accumulation of concrete is described as being a "battlefield without winners or losers." We cannot help asking ourselves if the whole thing is really some kind of alien cult site, or at least if it will be interpreted as such in a couple of decades.

Blick auf das Figurenfeld
View of the battlefield

Touristeninformation
Domplatz 8
85072 Eichstätt

p: 08421. 98800

f: 08421. 988030

e: tourismus@eichstaett.de

www.eichstaett.de

Germanischer Kunsttempel #1

Germanic Temple of Art #1

Der einstige Hexentanzplatz bei Thale wurde seit der Wende touristisch ausgeschlachtet. Nichts mehr lässt vermuten, dass sich hier einmal Menschen trafen, um im Mondschein zu tanzen und die Kräfte der Natur zu spüren. Weit abgelegen von den Wurstbuden und Automaten allerdings steht fast vergessen ein Kleinod – die 1901 von Hermann Hendrich und Bernhard Sehring gestaltete Walpurgishalle (mehr über Walburga S. 98).
Hendrich war ein Wagnerianer und großer Verehrer der deutschen Mythologie- und Sagenwelt. In seinen Bildern ließ er Nibelungen, Windsbräute, Drachen und Unterwelten in gespenstisches Licht getaucht wieder auferstehen. Er erwartete mehr von seinen Bildern, als in Museen ausgestellt zu werden. Herkömmliche Museen erschienen ihm als Orte künstlerischer Erstarrung. Und so schuf er zusammen mit Sehring einen eigenen Ort für seine Ausstellungsstücke, die Walpurgishalle. Nur dort, so Hendrichs Vision, können sie zur Geltung kommen und zum Leben erweckt werden. Große Natursteine tragen das dunkle Gebälk, über dem rustikalen Eingang thront Wotan, von zwei Raben umrankt. Die Halle umgibt eine natürliche Aura. Beim Eintreten passiert man einen alten Opferstein mit Sonnenrad, dann tritt man in die spärlich belichtete Halle mit ihrem modrigen Duft. Im ersten Raum hängt das Haupt eines Ziegenbocks, und auch den riecht man, zusammen mit den langsam verbleichenden Bildern. Irrlichter, die tanzen, Mephisto, das tote Gretchen und Urian. Im zweiten Raum ist zu DDR-Zeiten eine Ausstellung zum Hexenkult konzipiert worden: Miniaturfiguren stellen auf anschauliche Weise gängige Hexenrituale dar.
Verlässt man die Halle wieder, steht man im dunklen Wald und kann die Welt von Hendrichs Bildern regelrecht spüren.
Hendrich baute noch drei weitere Hallen, von denen aber nur noch eine erhalten ist: die Nibelungenhalle in Königswinter (siehe nächste Geschichte).

After the Berlin wall came down, the ancient Hexentanzplatz (witches dance square) close to Thale became a tourist magnet. Nothing here on top of the lone 401 m high rock reminds the visitor that people used to meet here, dancing in the moonlight, trying to get in touch with the forces of nature. Away from all the sausage stands and ticket booths, however, there is a nearly forgotten jewel waiting to be admired – the Walpurgis Hall, named after the famous Walpurga, who was later – due to her lasting popularity – turned into a Catholic saint (for more info please check story p. 98).
The Walpurgis Hall was designed by the painter Hermann Hendrich, who was a great admirer of Richard Wagner and of Germanic mythology in 1901. In his paintings, Hendrich depicted scenes from Germanic legends showing dragons, witches, heroes, virgins and dark figures from the underworld. Together with the architect Bernhard Sehring, the artist designed this hall as a home for his paintings.
The building is impressive. Heavy stone block columns support its dark wooden framework. Wotan, the highest Germanic god, is perched on top of the rustic entryway arch. On entering the hall, one passes by an ancient sun wheel engraved in a stone, which was probably once used for sacrificial rituals. In the first room, the skin of a goat hangs from a wooden beam. Its odor mixes with that of Hendrich's slowly fading paintings, which adorn the walls of the gloomily lit and musty main hall, all depicting scenes from Germanic witch legends. In the next room, there is an exhibit on witches and their history in the region, put together back in the time of the GDR. Miniature figures in glass cases portray various events in the daily life of a witch.
The visitor leaves the building, returning into the dark forest with a new feeling, inspired by Hendrich's mystic paintings. Hermann Hendrich designed three other halls as well, all dedicated to his paintings. Only two of these halls vhave been well-preserved. Have a read through the Nibelungen Halle (see next story).

Frontalansicht auf Walpurgishalle
Frontal view of Walpurgis Hall

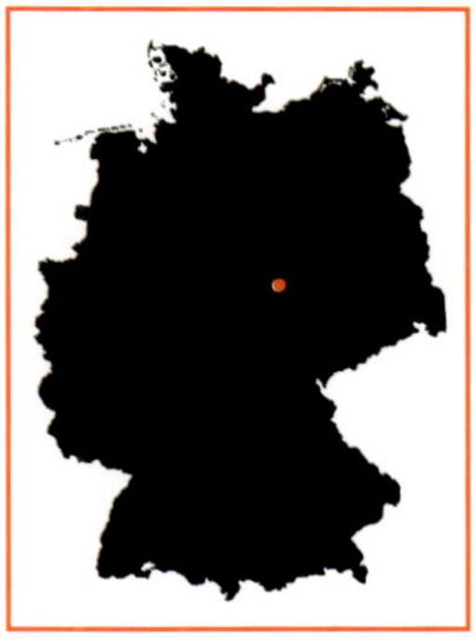

Walpurgishalle
Walpurgis Hall
Am Hexentanzplatz
06502 Thale

p: 03947. 2324

e: info@thale.de

www.harzer-bergtheater.de

Öffnungszeiten:
Mai bis Oktober:
täglich
9.00 – 17.00 Uhr

Opening hours:
May through October:
every day
9 am – 5 pm

Modell vom Treiben der Hexen in der Walpurgisnacht
Model showing what witches do on Walpurgis night

Hexe, die einen Stein wegrollt
Witch rolling a stone away

No Entrance!
Attention: Tournament Crocodiles

Germanischer Kunsttempel #2
Germanic Temple of Art #2

Der Drachenfels war noch in den 50er und 60er Jahren eines der beliebtesten Ausflugsziele der Deutschen. Millionen von Menschen – Schulklassen, Familien und Betriebsausflügler – hielten mit dem Bus unterhalb des Felsens und schleppten sich hoch zur Burg, von der aus man eine weite Rheinschlaufe übersehen kann.
Seit 1913 kreuzt man auf diesem Weg die Nibelungenhalle – ein von Hermann Hendrichs konzipierter Tempel, der seine Bilder beheimatet. Die Bilder stellen Szenen der von Wagner vertonten Nibelungensage dar. Die Nibelungenhalle erinnert schon alleine vom Bau an die Welt der Sagen. Die Mischung aus Jugendstil, Art Deco und Klassizismus unterstreicht ihren weihevollen Charakter. Zahlenmystik, eine Midgardschlange und das Firmament des nordischen Himmels tauchen die Bilder in eine eigene Atmosphäre. Der Platz ist gut gewählt, denn genau hier soll der Drache Fafnir, den Siegfried auf seinem Weg durchs Siebengebirge besiegte, gelebt haben. Deshalb befindet sich hinter der Halle auch ein Abbild des Drachen sowie ein kleiner Reptilienzoo – alles das wird auch heute noch aus privater Hand finanziert. Das Konzept der Halle – ein Lobgesang auf die germanische Kultur – wurde, angesichts des Germanenkultes im Dritten Reich, in den letzten 50 Jahren oft missverstanden, so dass kaum Gelder für die Instandhaltung ge-

In the 1950's and 60's, the Drachenfels (Dragon's Rock) was one of the most popular day trip destinations in Germany. Millions of people, entire school classes, families, colleagues and clubs all came by bus to walk up to the castle on top of the rock and enjoy the view of the Rhine river.
It is halfway up to the top of Dragon's Rock that you will find the "Nibelungen Hall," built in 1913. The hall is dedicated to Richard Wagner, and to the paintings of Hermann Hendrich. Hendrich's paintings depict scenes from the Germanic legends, the Nibelungen. The Nibelungen were also an important theme in the work of composer Richard Wagner and played a significant role in the creation of the German identity, at least until about 1944.
Hendrich also designed the hall, with its unique and solemn architectural expression, a mixture of Art Deco and Classicism. The use of numbers, the mosaic of a Midgard snake, and the ceiling painting of the Nordic starry sky lend a mystic quality to this temple of art. The location was carefully selected. According to the legend, a dragon called Fafnir once lived in the place. The dragon was defeated by Siegfried, the hero of the Nibelungen legend.
In memorial to the dragon, a giant statue of him lies slumbering at the back of the hall, where there is also a small private reptile zoo to peruse.

Eingang zur Nibelungenhalle
Entrance to the Nibelungen Hall

funden werden konnten. Positiv zu bewerten dabei ist, dass gerade das Fehlen von deutschem Perfektionismus in der Renovierung ihren einzigartigen Charme untermalt.
Heute ist die Hauptattraktion der Halle der Reptilienzoo: alles Nachfahren Fafnirs!

Both the hall and the zoo are run privately by a single lady, who is now having a difficult time. After the Nazi misuse of Germanic heroes and traditions for their propaganda, public interest is low, and the state refuses to support art dealing with this theme. Maybe it is exactly the lack of shiny state supported perfectionism, however, that gives the place its unique charm.

Der Drache Fafnir
Fafnir the Dragon

Stummer Wächter aus Stein
Silent sentry made of stone

Nibelungenhalle
The Nibelungen Hall
Drachenfelsstrasse 107
53639 Königswinter

p: 02223. 24150

www.reptilien-zoo-koenigs-winter.de

Öffnungszeiten:
Im Sommer:
täglich
10.00 – 18.00 Uhr
Im Winter:
Sa und So
10.30 – 16.00 Uhr

Opening hours:
In summer:
every day
10 am – 6 pm
In winter:
Sat and Sun
10.30 am – 4 pm

FULL
FULL

Märchen

Fairy Tales

Eingang zur Märchenhöhle
The entrance to the fairy-tale cave

Verborgene Märchen
Hidden Fairy Tales

Versteckt unter einer zweitklassigen Minigolfanlage und hinter einer Armada von automatischen Kinderspielzeugen befindet sich der Eingang zu einem wahren Juwel: der größten Sandsteinhöhle Nordeuropas – die Sandstein- und Märchenhöhle Walldorf.
Tagelöhner gruben hier seit dem Mittelalter den weichen Sandstein ab – sie gewannen daraus den feinen Scheuersand, der zum Waschen von Geschirr oder dem Schmirgeln von Holz verwendet wurde. Tag um Tag verbrachten sie im Dunklen und gruben mit der Zeit 2500 Säulen frei, die das Gewölbe stützen. Es entstand ein von Menschenhand geschaffenes Höhlensystem.
Sogenannte Sandmänner zogen mit dem Lied „Der Sandmann ist da, er hat so schönen weißen Sand, ist allen Leuten wohlbekannt…“ von Stadt zu Stadt und priesen den schwer erarbeiteten Scheuersand an.
Das ging bis zum Ersten Weltkrieg so. Dann lohnte sich der Aufwand nicht mehr. Eine Zeit lang versuchte man in den Höhlen Champignons zu züchten, aber es war zu warm. Zu DDR-Zeiten entdeckten die Kinder des Ortes die Höhlen für sich – Teile der Höhlen waren inzwischen mit Wasser gefüllt, darauf ließ sich klasse Boot fahren. In den trockenen Teilen führten die Kinder Theaterstücke auf. 1957

Hidden beneath a second-rate miniature golf park, behind an assemblage of automatic children's toys, lies the entrance to a true jewel: the biggest sandstone cave in Northern Europe, the "Sandstone and Fairy Tale Cave Walldorf."
Workers began digging at the soft sandstone here back in the Middle Ages. They were toiling for the very fine Scheuersand, or scrubbing sand, that was used to clean dishes or polish wood surfaces. Digging deeper into the darkness over the many years, they eventually created some 2,500 sandstone columns, which now support the cave system.
So called "Sandmänner" moved from town to town singing, "The sandman is here, he's got such nice white sand, and everybody knows it…" trying to sell their wares.
This tradition continued up until the First World War, when, seen as too strenuous under modern conditions, the old custom died out. For a while, people tried growing mushrooms in the caves, but it was too warm there, and the attempt failed. In the GDR times, the children of Walldorf discovered the caves for themselves. Parts of the cave were filled with water, allowing for excellent boat travel. In dryer parts, the children put on plays and skits. In 1957, the grown-ups of Walldorf began to join in, setting up

Gulliver
Gulliver

In der Höhle
In the cave

begannen die Walldorfer in den vielen Höhlengewölben Märchen mit Figuren nachzustellen, dann die Geschichte der Tagelöhner und schließlich ein paar Höhlenmonster. Heute führt ein Weg durch die Höhlen – der ideale Ort für Märchenlaune.

fairy tale scenes with miniature figures in some of the cave's chambers. Shortly after, they had another idea and decided to tell the story of the day laborers who had worked in the mines, finally even setting up a couple of cave monsters. Today there is a little path leading through the cave – the ideal place for fairy tale ambience.

Die Sieben Schwaben
The Seven Swabians

Walldorf um 1840
Walldorf in 1840

Sandstein- und Märchenhöhle
Sandstone Fairy Tale Cave
98639 Walldorf

p: 03693. 89910

f: 03693. 890163

e: sandsteinhoehle@t-online.de

Öffnungszeiten:
1. März bis 1. November
täglich
9.00 – 16.30 Uhr

Opening hours:
March 1st to November 1st:
daily
9 am – 4.30 pm

Das Schlaraffenland
Beyond the Candy Mountain

Rotkäppchen
Little Red Riding Hood

Die Geburtsstätte der Gartenzwerge

Birthplace of the Garden Gnome

Woher kommt der Gartenzwerg? Der Exportschlager der DDR und das Markenzeichen der deutschen Vorgartenidylle kommt konkret aus einem kleinen Ort in Thüringen: Gräfenroda. Hier gibt es seit vier Generationen den Gartenzwergbetrieb der Familie Griebel. Philip Griebel, der Begründer der Griebel Dynastie war „Thierkopfmodelleur". Zu seinen Lebzeiten, der Biedermeierzeit, galt es im Bürgertum als chique, einen realistisch modellierten Hirschkopf als Wandschmuck zu besitzen. Philip Griebel gründete seinen eigenen Betrieb, suchte aber nach neuen Motiven – Rehe, Märchenfiguren und dann endlich, die Gartenzwerge. Auf der Messe in Leipzig 1884 wurde das neue Produkt dann prompt vorgestellt und auch bestellt. Der Erste Weltkrieg ließ die Produktion einschlafen, sie wurde dann aber wieder aufgegriffen und auch der Zweite Weltkrieg konnte die fleißigen Gartenzwergmanufakteure nicht lahm legen. Nur zu DDR-Zeiten wurde ein zeitweises Verbot erlassen – bis man bemerkte, dass die kleinen Wichtel im Ausland harte Devisen einbrachten. Der Betrieb wurde wieder in Gang gesetzt und aufgestockt: 23 Mitarbeiter modellierten täglich an einer ganzen Armee von Gartenzwergen, die nach Skandinavien, Westdeutschland und sogar bis nach Amerika hin verkauft wurden.

Heute ist Reinhard Griebel der Besitzer der Manufaktur. Er kann gerade mal zwei Helfer einstellen, die Arbeitskräfte sind teurer geworden. Dennoch ist er frohen Mutes: er hat ein Museum gebaut, das die Geschichte und Produktentwicklung der Gartenzwerge dokumentiert und verkauft neuerdings sogar über das Internet.

Where does the garden gnome actually come from? The leading export article of the late GDR and the hallmark of German front lawn decoration does in fact have a genuine place of birth: Gräfenroda, Thuringia. The family owned garden gnome manufacturer Griebel is now in its fourth generation. The dynasty's founder, Phillip Griebel, began by molding ceramic animal busts. During his lifetime, also referred to as the Biedermeier period, it was considered chic among the bourgeoisie to own a life-like-modelled stag's head as wall decoration. Griebel founded his own company and began looking for new motifs. Beginning with deer, he moved on to fairy tale figures and finally ended up with the now world-renowned garden gnome. The product was introduced to the market for the first time at a fair in Leipzig in 1884. Orders immediately started pouring in.

During the First World War, production was halted for a time, but was quickly back up and running again. Not even the Second World War could hold back the popular product. In the early days of the eastern sector, the GDR saw potential problems with the Gnomes, and issued a ban on them, but not for long. It was quickly realized that these little men had the potential to earn big cash abroad. Production started up again, this time on a large scale. 23 workers modelled an entire army of gnomes every day. These were sold in Scandinavia, West Germany, and even in America.

The current owner of the production plant is Reinhard Griebel. Though he can barely afford employing two modellers, he is in good spirits. He has built a museum telling the history of the gnomes and has recently started selling them over the internet.

Gartenzwerge
Ohrdrufer Str. 1
99330 Gräfenroda

p: 036205. 76470

e: reinhard.griebel@zwergen-griebel.de

Öffnungszeiten:
Mo bis Fr
10.00 – 17.00 Uhr
Sa
10.00 – 14.00 Uhr
1. April – 25. Oktober:
auch So
10.00 – 14.00 Uhr

Opening hours:
Mon to Fri
10 am – 5 pm
Sat
10 am – 2 pm
April 1st – October 25th:
also Sun
10 am – 2 pm

Alte Zwerge, neue Zwerge und Zwerge, die noch welche werden
Old gnomes, new gnomes, and gnomes in waiting

Kalifornien
California

Kalifornien ist in Deutschland. Von wegen „it never rains“! Wer hierher angelockt wird, plumpst geradewegs in die Ostsee, ganz ohne spektakulären Sonnenuntergang.
Anstatt der Wale gibt es hier Quallen, anstatt Flowerpower ein „Ostseefestival der Countrymusik“.
Gemein hat das deutsche Kalifornien mit seinem amerikanischen Counterpart, dass auch hier die Freiheit groß geschrieben wird: Kalifornien liegt in der Probstei, ein Fleckchen Schleswig-Holstein, in dem es keine Leibeigenen gab. Alle Bauern hier waren frei und eine handvoll Auswanderer, angezogen von diesem Versprechen, gab es auch.
Wie kommt der Ort zu seinem Namen? Das große Kalifornien war zuerst da. Wann das kleine in der Probstei entstand, weiß heute so sicher keiner mehr. Der in Kalifornien lebende Märchenerzähler Georg Kulick, angelockt von den günstigen Immobilienpreisen und dem Slogan „Leben, wo andere Ferien machen“, hat folgende Geschichte zu berichten: Ein Fischer baute sich am Strand eine Hütte. Das Strandgut lieferte das Holz dafür. Darunter auch ein Brett mit der Aufschrift Kalifornien, wahrscheinlich der Name eines gesunkenen Schiffes. Da zu diesen Zeiten Kalifornien gleich stand mit dem Goldrausch und dem damit verbundenen großen Glück, nagelte der Fischer das Brett vor seine Hütte. Fortan war das hier Kalifornien.
Heute steht hier eines der über 200 Eisenbahn-Museen Deutschlands, der Strand lädt zu langen Spaziergängen ein. Nach Brasilien ist es übrigens nur einen Katzensprung: So heißt eine Gemeinde unweit von Kalifornien.

California is in Germany. Admittedly, the “it never rains in” does not quite fit in this case. Those who are allured to this part of the country are in danger of falling right into the Baltic Sea, however, which is quite a bit colder than the Pacific Ocean, and does not have quite as spectacular a sunset. Instead of whales on the horizon you will find jellyfish on the shoreline; instead of flower power, an annual Baltic Country Music festival.
Yet, this place does have something in common with its American sister. Freedom is spelled in capital letters here. California belongs to a stretch of land called the Probstei. This is a part of Schleswig-Holstein, and, unlike other regions, it has never had bond-slaves or peasants. All farmers were free here, and there were even a couple of settlers who traveled here, attracted by the promise of freedom.
How did the place get its name? Though it is certain that the bigger California was first, nobody knows anymore exactly when this smaller one came into being. California resident and storyteller Georg Kulick, who was attracted to the place by one of its slogans, “to live where others spend their holidays,” had the following story to tell: A fisherman had built a hut out of driftwood near the beach. Amongst the wood was a plank with the word California written on it, probably part of a sunken ship. As in these days, California was known as a metaphor for gold, riches, and good fortune, he happily used the plank for his house, nailing it onto the front wall with the sign’s lettering facing outwards. In this way, a part of the Baltic Sea’s coast became California.
Today, one of the more than 200 train museums in Germany can be found in California. The ocean calls out to its visitors, inviting them for long walks on the beach. Brasilia is also not too far away: this is the name of another town just a ways down the coast.

Das Ortsschild von Kalifornien
California's city limits sign

24217 Kalifornien/Schönberg

25 km nordöstlich entfernt von Kiel
25 km from Kiel in northeast direction

Am Strand von Kalifornien
On the beach in California

Schwäbisches Disneyland
Swabian Disneyland

Albert Schöchle, der schwäbische Walt Disney, kannte sich aus im Bauen von urdeutschen Familienattraktionen: vor dem Zweiten Weltkrieg hatte er die Wilhelma, den Stuttgarter Zoo, geleitet. Zur Zeit des deutschen Wirtschaftswunders gestaltete er den Park beim Schloss Ludwigsburg zu einem attraktiven Familienausflugsziel um – dem sogenannten Blühenden Barock. Es fehlte nur noch eine Attraktion für die Kleinen. In Holland in der Nähe von Tillberg ließ er sich von einem Märchengarten inspirieren und beschloss, einen ebensolchen in Ludwigsburg aufzubauen. Zwei Jahre lang musste er die Beamten der Stadt von seinen Plänen überzeugen – ein Märchengarten, im Blühenden Barock! Schöchle, der in seiner Biografie als „Schlitzohr" beschrieben wird, überreichte 1959 den Garten der Stadt. Dieser wurde sofort begeistert angenommen.
Bis heute hat der Park sich kaum verändert, wurde nur um das ein oder andere Märchen ergänzt, so dass hier mittlerweile 40 Attraktionen zu finden sind. Die Klassiker gibt es hier allemal: einen alten Turm muss man mit „Rapunzel, lass dein Haar herunter" anbrüllen und schon kommt von oben ein flachsgelber Zopf herunter – nicht ohne deutlich hörbares Motorengeknatter. In einem ehemaligen Verlies haust der Rübezahl und lacht den Besucher schallend aus. Verstreut im Garten sind verzauberte Fliegenpilze, die Wünsche erfüllen, und selbst die Papierkörbe sind verzauberte Drachen, die flüstern: „Hunger, Papier." Jedes Märchen kommt nur in Fahrt, wenn die Kinder selbst etwas dazu beitragen: Entweder müssen sie eine Türklinke drücken, ein Sprüchlein aufsagen oder etwas vorsingen. Das Schöne daran: Die Technik ist immer noch auf dem Stand der 50er Jahre und funktioniert genauso verlässlich, wie man sich darauf verlassen kann, dass sich die Kinder auch heute noch für die Märchen begeistern. Sehr schön ist auch die schwäbische Hexe: „Knuschper, Knuschper, Knäusle, wer knuschpert an meinarem Häusle?"

Albert Schöchle, the Swabian answer to Walt Disney, was very experienced when it came to building family attractions. Before WWII, he had managed the Wilhelma, Stuttgart's famous and popular zoo. After the war, as the German economic miracle was in full swing, he designed the Chateau Park in Ludwigsburg, transforming it into an appealing family resort, named the Blühendes Baroque, or Blooming Baroque. It was almost the perfect family retreat. All that was missing was an attraction for children. He finally found his inspiration in the Netherlands, in a fairy tale park not far from Tillberg, and decided to create something similar in Ludwigsburg. His only problem was that he still had to convince the local bureaucrats to support the project. Described as being a "chisel" in his biography, he spent the next two years pleading with his superiors to help finance his Fairy Tale Garden in the Blooming Baroque. In 1959 he was finally able to open the garden to the public, and it was an immediate success.
The park has not changed much since its opening. A couple of new attractions have been added, making over 40 different fairy tale experiences in all. All the German classics are here. When you shout towards a dark old tower, "Rapunzel, Rapunzel, let down your hair," the captured Rapunzel lowers her long golden locks, just as it is in the Brother Grimms' story. "The Star Coin," another Grimms' classic is also to be enjoyed here. When you press a button, a beautiful girl collects falling stars in her skirt. Another must see is the famous Ali Baba's Cave, which opens only to the call, "Open Sesame!"
Each fairy tale is activated through interaction with the children. Sometimes they have to open a door, sometimes press down a handle, other times they have to sing a song or recite a slogan. The old 50's technology is still used in the park, working marvelously and adding to its charm. This park will be a hit for as long as kids are still elated by fairy tales. Our favorite was the witch from "Hansel and Gretel," who spoke in a heavy Swabian accent.

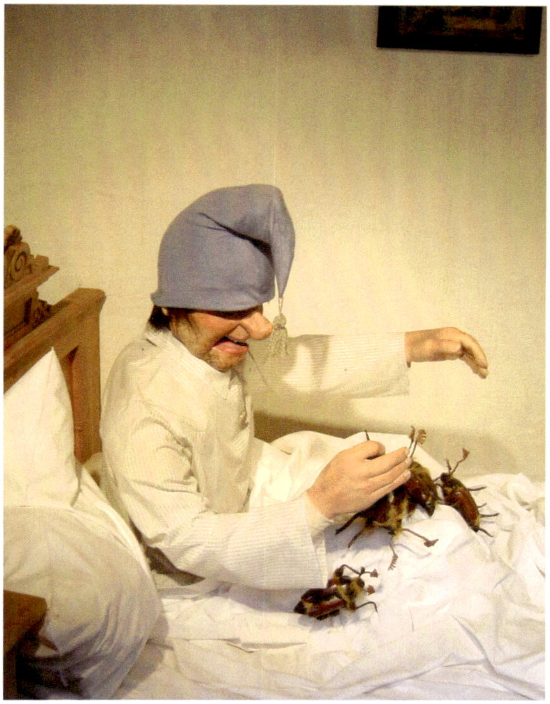

Alte Bekannte aus der Kindheit
Old childhood acquaintances

Märchengarten im Blühenden Barock
Fairy Tale Garden
Im Park des Schlosses
In the Castle Park
Mömpelgardstraße 28
71640 Ludwigsburg

p: 07141. 975650

f: 07141. 9756533

Öffnungszeiten:
Täglich
9.00 – 18.00 Uhr.
Nach dem 3. Oktober täglich
10.00 – 17.00 Uhr
Von Anfang November bis Ende März geschlossen

Opening Hours:
Every day
9 am – 6 pm
After October 3rd every day
10 am – 5 pm
Closed from the beginning of November till end of March

Der Lügenbaron

The Baron of Lies

Es hat ihn wirklich gegeben – den Lügenbaron Hieronymus von Münchhausen: Er wurde am 11. Mai 1720 in Bodenwerder an der Weser geboren. Seine Sturm- und Drangjahre verbrachte er im Türkenkrieg, in Finnland und in St. Petersburg. Orte, die später in seinen Lügengeschichten wieder auftauchen. Nach vielen Abenteuern kehrte Münchhausen 1750 wieder zurück nach Bodenwerder, und da es dort weit langweiliger war, als an seinen anderen Aufenthaltsorten, lebte er fortan in ewigem Streit mit den Bürgern Bodenwerders.

Münchhausen war ein wahres Erzählgenie und ließ sogar oberhalb seines Hauses ein Grottenhäuschen bauen, in dem er viele Stunden mit Wein und vor Gästen seine unglaublichen Geschichten zum Besten geben konnte. Aufgeschrieben hatte er sie allerdings nie. Das tat ein gewisser Raspe 1785 in England, wo Münchhausens Geschichten sofort bekannt und noch zu Lebzeiten des Barons ins Deutsche übersetzt wurden. Zu jenem Zeitpunkt ärgerte sich der Baron gerade mit der Scheidung von seiner 56 Jahre jüngeren Frau herum, und es passte ihm gar nicht, als Lügenbaron bekannt zu werden.

Heute kann man in seinem Geburtshaus ein Zimmer besuchen, in dem verschiedene Figuren seiner Erzählungen und Gebrauchsartikel von ihm zu sehen sind, so auch der Hase mit den acht Beinen – zwei Paar oben und zwei Paar unten, falls eine Seite müde werden sollte.

Ganz besonders reizend ist die ältere Dame, die sich des Museums angenommen hat. An Sonntagen lädt sie ins Grottenhäuschen, um dort nach alter Manier bei Wein die guten Geschichten wieder aufleben zu lassen.

He really did exist! – The famous "Baron of Lies," Hieronymus von Münchhausen. Born on May 11th 1720 in Bodenwerder, the young Münchhausen spent his stormy youth as a soldier in the war against Turkey, fighting in Finland, and perusing through St. Petersburg. After many years of adventure in far away places, Münchhausen returned to his hometown in 1750 where he soon became bored by the life and people there, getting entangled in endless quarrels with his fellow citizens.

Münchhausen had a great talent for story telling and used this to chase away his boredom and frustration. Near his home, up on a hill, the Baron had a fantastical grotto house built. Here he spent hours upon hours serving wine and entertaining guests with the most unbelievable of stories.

Unfortunately, Münchhausen himself never wrote his stories down. This was done however, by a Mr. Raspe, a well-connected researcher who had probably been little more than an acquaintance to the Baron. The stories were actually published anonymously and without permission from Münchhausen. In 1785, Raspe published "Baron Münchhausen's Narrative of his Marvelous Travels and Campaigns in Russia" in England, where the book became instantly popular. Shortly thereafter, the stories were published in German and became a phenomenon in the Baron's home country as well. The Baron, who was entwined in a painful divorce suite with his 56 years younger wife at the time, was not pleased to have become known as the "Baron of Lies," as this did not seem to help his case.

Today, the old children's room in the Baron's house is dedicated to his infamous whoppers. Some of the objects described in his stories are on display there. You can see a rabbit with 8 legs – four regular ones, and four on its back. According to legend, if the rabbit's legs got tired, he could flip around and use the top ones! A nice middle-aged lady takes care of the museum. On Sundays, selected guests are invited up to the grotto house where, in the old tradition, stories are told and wine is served.

Brunnen in Bodenwerder
The well in Bodenwerder

Das Grottenhäuschen
The Grotto-House

Der achtbeinige Hase
The eight-legged rabbit

Der Ritt auf der Kanonenkugel
The great cannon ball ride

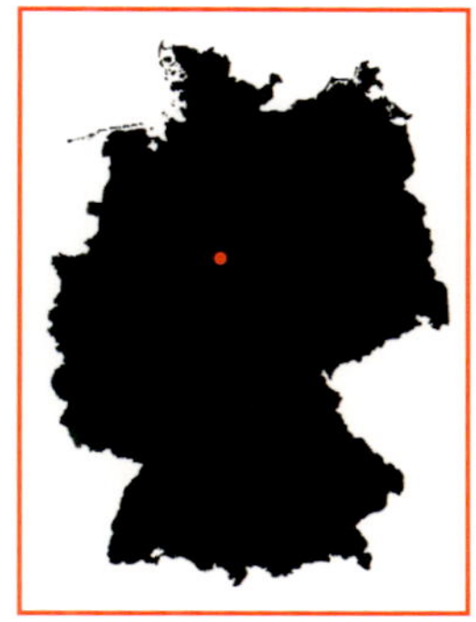

Das Münchhausenzimmer
Baron von Münchhausen's Room
Münchhausenplatz 1
37619 Bodenwerder

p: 05533. 4050

Öffnungszeiten:
April bis Oktober:
täglich
10.00 – 12.00 Uhr und
14.00 – 17.00 Uhr
Im Winter nach Vereinbarung

Opening hours:
April to October:
daily
10 am – noon and
2 pm – 5 pm
In winter by appointment only

Naturspiel

Freak of Nature

Das Bodenlose Loch
The Bottomless Pit

Die reiche Kulturlandschaft Frankens ist voll von kleinen Schlossanlagen, mittelalterlichen Dörfern, heiligen Orten und Heimatkundemuseen. Und in der Gemeinde Diebach gibt es sogar ein „Bodenloses Loch". Leider ist das Bodenlose Loch so klein, dass man zweimal dran vorbeifährt. Nur ein schon fast verrottetes Schild bei Oestheim weist auf einen Feldweg in die Richtung des Lochs. Schönes Detail: Das Schild ist mit fränkischem Rechtschreibfehler versehen: Zum bodenlose Loch.

Wie hat man sich ein „Bodenloses Loch" vorzustellen? Dass es sich bei dem Loch um eine Quelle handelt, macht die Sache auch nicht leichter. Steht man aber einmal davor und schaut in das mit Wasserpflanzen überwachsene Loch hinein, überkommt einen ein kleines Schaudern – es scheint tatsächlich bodenlos zu sein. Der Tümpel erscheint einem wirklich sehr tief; das Wasser verfärbt sich vom Türkisblau ins dunkelste Dunkelblau. In Oestheim munkelt man, dass das Loch gar bis nach Amerika reiche! Und einmal soll hier ein ganzes Schloss versunken sein. Gar nicht wahr, sagt der Bürgermeister: In Wirklichkeit wohnen hier die Meerjungfrauen, die auch im Wappen der Gemeinde zu finden sind. Und stets gingen sie mit den Burschen zum Tanz. Als sie einmal zu spät zu ihrem Loch zurückkamen, verfärbte

The culturally rich landscape of the Franken region is littered with small castles, medieval villages, holy places and local history museums. The district of Diebach even has a bottomless pit. Unfortunately, the pit is so small, that it is almost impossible to find. A half-rotten sign, right at the border of Oestheim, points to a narrow field path that leads to the pit. A nice detail: There is a spelling mistake on the sign, derived from the local dialect.

How does one fathom such a bottomless pit? The fact that the pit is actually a well-spring does not make it any easier. Standing over the hole and looking into its water filled, and with plants overgrown abyss, does produce a shiver though. The color of the water turns, the deeper it goes, from a brilliant turquoise to the darkest deepest blue.

The people of Oestheim say that the pit goes all the way down to America, and that once, an entire castle sank down into its endless depths. "Completely wrong," says the mayor. "The truth of the matter is that mermaids live there." These mermaids adorn Diebach's coat of arms. They used to leave their pit late at night to go dancing with the boys in town. Once, they came home too late, with dramatic consequences: the water turned blood red, and the mermaids were never seen again.

Eingebettet in die idyllische Landschaft Frankens: das Bodenlose Loch
Nestled in the idyllic Franconian countryside: the bottomless pit

sich das Wasser rot und seitdem waren sie nicht mehr gesehen …
Viel gibt es nicht zu beachten, außer, dass man in der Weihnachtsnacht nicht am Loch vorbeifahren solle. Das hat einmal ein Bäuerlein getan und versank mit Wagen und Pferden im Bodenlosen. Daraufhin wurde ein Zaun um das Loch gebaut, doch der existiert schon lange nicht mehr. Jetzt wiegen Weiden ihre Äste um das Loch und im Loch wiegen die Wasserpflanzen mit dem Quellfluss.

There is not too much else you need to know about the pit. Just make sure not to drive by on Christmas Eve. A farmer did this with his horse and wagon once, and sank into the bottomless depths. Thereafter, a fence was built up around the hole, but this does not exist anymore. Now, the willows around it are lulling their branches to sleep. In the pit itself, various plants are dozing and drifting in the current of the spring water.

Schild mit „Sprachfehler"
Sign with "spelling mistake"

Die Untiefen des Bodenlosen Lochs
The amazing depths of the bottomless pit

Bodenloses Loch
Auf der Heilingerwiese
In Heilinger Field
91583 Diebach-Oestheim

50er Jahre Charme erwartet den Besucher schon an der Kasse
1950's charm awaits the visitor even at the ticket counter

Mineralbad Berg
Mineral Spa Berg

Ein wahrer Jungbrunnen ist das Mineralbad Berg in Stuttgart. Seit 1856 im Familienbesitz sprudeln auch heute noch täglich 5 Millionen Liter kohlensäurehaltiges Nass. Bei so viel Wasser wird auf Chlorierung oder Umwälzung verzichtet – Badevergnügen für Puristen. Mit seinen nur 18 Grad ist das Baden zwar gewöhnungsbedürftig, doch ist man erst mal drin, fühlt man sich durch das zusätzliche leichte Prickeln des Wassers wach, munter und aufgeweckt.
Seit den 50er Jahren des 20. Jahrhunderts wurde hier nicht viel renoviert, die Umkleidekabinen sind aus Holz mit einer raffinierten Verschließtechnik, die noch aus den Zeiten des deutschen Wirtschaftswunders stammt. Auch die Stammgäste sind dieselben wie damals. Man flaniert durch den im Gelsenkirchener Barock angelegten Park, spielt Schach neben dem Imbiss oder bräunt sich auf den hölzernen Planken, die das Becken umgeben. Im Winter kann man auch auf ein Innenbecken ausweichen und sich dort in alten Messingtrögen baden.
Die Ruhe im Mineralbad Berg ist auffällig. Niemand planscht oder spritzt herum, der Besitzer sagt stolz: „Hier schwimmt man nicht, hier badet man." Selbst am Abend, wenn das Bad schließt, nimmt man Rücksicht auf die er-

The Mineralbad (Mineral Spa) Berg, in Stuttgart, is a true fountain of youth. Over 5 million litres of water spurt from the spa's spring every day, eliminating the need for chlorination or agitation – this is Badvergnügen, or bathing pleasure, for purists. With a temperature of only 18 degrees Celsius, it takes some coaxing to get in, but once in the water, you feel immediately invigorated, due in part to a slight prickling sensation.
Family owned since 1856, the spa has looked the same since the 1950's. Nothing has been changed. The dressing rooms are made of massive wood boards (be careful not to get a splinter) and have an interesting closing mechanism. The doors are closed by pulling down a bench. Even the regular guests have not changed since the 50's. In the spa, one can stroll through the fake baroque park, play a game of chess in front of the Imbiss (the German answer to fast food), or get a tan on the wooden planks next to the pool. In winter, guests prefer to use the indoor pool, maybe enjoying a bath in one of the old brass tubs there.
The silence in the spa is remarkable. There is no jumping or splashing around. The owner says, not without a trace of pride, "People do not swim here, they bathe." Even in the

Ein herrliches Badevergnügen im 18 Grad Celsius kalten Wasser
Marvelous bathing enjoyment in 18°C cold water

holten Gäste: zum Ende des Badetages wird hier das Lied „Auf Wiedersehen" von Vera Lynn aus den Lautsprechern gespielt.

evening, when the spa is closing, guests' relaxation comes first: The slightly melancholy and calming song, "Auf Wiedersehen," by Vera Lynn, plays gently, announcing the end of another day at the mineral spa Berg, in Stuttgart.

Die Umkleidekabinen im Mineralbad Berg
The changing-rooms at the Berg Mineral Bath Spa

Mineralbad Berg
Berg Mineral Baths
Am Schwanenplatz 9
70190 Stuttgart

p: 0711. 9236516

Öffnungszeiten:
Mo bis Do
6.00 – 20.00 Uhr
Fr bis Sa
6.00 – 21.00 Uhr
So
6.00 – 17.00 Uhr

Opening hours:
Mon to Thu
6 am – 8 pm
Fri to Sat
6 am – 9 pm
Sun
6 am – 5 pm

Der letzte Urwald

The Last Ancient Forest

Einer der letzten Urwälder Deutschlands erstreckt sich um das Schloss, in dem einst Dornröschen gehaust haben soll – der Sabawald bei der Sababurg.

Hier stehen alte Eichen und Buchen: Die knorrige Kamineiche ist sogar über 800 Jahre alt. Man kann den natürlich belassenen Wald auf einem kleinen Wanderweg durchqueren und muss immer wieder über das üppige Wachstum staunen. Wenn abends die Sonne hinter den alten Bäumen untergeht und die Farne das Licht brechen, versteht man die Faszination der Märchenwelt, von der die Gebrüder Grimm im nahen Kassel gepackt waren.

Der Sabawald war nicht immer Urwald: Was man heute von ihm sieht, ist nur noch die historische Form eines Wirtschaftswaldes: Der Sabawald diente seit dem 30-Jährigen Krieg der Viehzucht, war also ein Hutewald, ein Wald, in dem Tiere gehütet wurden. Damals schlug man die Eichen und Buchen frei, um mehr Eicheln und Bucheckern für das Vieh zu haben. In einem Reglement von 1630 steht, dass in diesem Hutewald 20 000 Schafe, 6 000 Schweine, 6 000 Rinder, 3 000 Pferde, 700 Ziegen und 50 Packesel gehütet wurden.

Anfang des 20. Jahrhunderts, als neue Methoden in der Tierhaltung die Landwirtschaft revolutionierten, war der Hutewald plötzlich out: Tiere wurden jetzt im Stall gehalten und so konnte eine zu einseitige Art der Forstwirtschaft gerade noch verhindert werden. Die meisten Hutewälder verschwanden, nur der Sabawald wurde sich selbst überlassen. Seit über 80 Jahren wird dieser Wald von keinem Förster oder Jäger gepflegt und hat dadurch seine urwaldähnliche Ausstrahlung erhalten. Daher Vorsicht: Wer sich von den schmalen Wanderpfaden entfernt, läuft Gefahr, dass ihm ein morscher Ast auf den Kopf fällt.

One of the last ancient forests in Germany is stretched around the castle in which Sleeping Beauty is supposed to have lived – the Sabawald (Saba Forest) around the Sababurg (Saba Castle).

Old oaks and beeches slumber peacefully here. The knotty and gnarled "Chimney Oak" is over 800 years old. Wandering down a small path through this untouched world of natural wonders, one gapes in astonishment at the giant vegetation. As the sun goes down behind the aged trees and breaks through the ferns, one begins to understand the fascination of the fairytale world from which the Brothers Grimm from nearby Kassel were so enchanted.

The Saba Forest was not always an ancient forest. What you see today is the remains of a planned wood. After the Thirty Years War, the wood served as a holding and breeding ground for livestock. The animals could roam freely here, eating as much as they pleased. The farmers of the time used to clear the woods of everything but oaks and beech trees, so that there would be more acorns and beechnuts for use as fodder. In a document from 1630, it is written that in this herding wood, there were 20,000 sheep, 6,000 pigs, 6,000 cows, 3,000 horses, 700 goats, and 50 donkeys herded together.

At the beginning of the 20th century, as new methods revolutionized practices in animal husbandry and agriculture, the herding woods became obsolete. Animals were instead held in stalls, barely hindering a too one-sided procedure in forestry from wreaking havoc. Most of these herding woods then disappeared. Only the Saba Forest was left to itself. The forest has not been touched by a ranger, woodsman, gamekeeper, or hunter for over 80 years. Therefore, be careful: Whoever wanders off from the narrow path may be hit on the head by an old rotten branch.

Urwald Sababurg
(im Reinhardswald)
Ancient Forest Sababurg
(in Reinhard's Forest)
34369 Hofgeismar

Der Druidenhain
The Druids' Grove

Die keltischen Ortsnamen der Umgebung lassen darauf schließen, dass hier vor 2500 Jahren tatsächlich einmal Kelten gelebt haben müssen. So verwundert es auch nicht weiter, wenn die geometrische Anhäufung von 364 moosbewachsenen Steinen im dunklen Wald bei Wohlmannsgesees von Esoterikern als druidischer Kultplatz der Kelten gedeutet wird. Mystisch ist der Ort allemal. Aber ob er darum wirklich die Kräfte hat, die man ihm nachsagt, ist ungewiss. Die Steine haben Namen wie „Taufstein", „Opferstein", „Altar". Der "Pultstein" am Eingang neigt sich um 51,5 Grad, was genau der Neigung der Pyramiden entspricht. Die Anzahl der Steine gleicht den Tagen im keltischen Kalender.

Die Nazis haben im Zuge ihrer „Germanenforschung" hier viel erprobt und angeblich die kosmische Energie eines der Steine direkt an Hitler weitergeleitet. Darum findet man heute viele „weise" Frauen und Männer, die auf Erdheilungsseminaren die Kraft der Steine wieder „reinigen". Genauso findet man schwarzgekleidete, ungesund aussehende junge Menschen, die im Kerzenschein seltsame Worte murmeln. Was man aber nicht findet, sind Anzeichen, dass hier wirklich einmal Druiden getagt haben – weder durch Ausgrabungen noch durch Runen in den Steinen. Wissenschaftler haben außerdem herausgefunden, dass die Felsformation des Druidenhains auf die natürliche geologische Ausprägung der Umgebung zurückzuführen ist.

Ein Bewohner von Wohlmannsgesees aber erzählte uns, dass es den Druidenhain dennoch gibt – nur an einer anderen Stelle. Als junger Mann hatte er hier unter einem Fels gebuddelt und ein goldenes Armband und andere Ritualgegenstände gefunden. Diese gab er an den Dorfpolizisten weiter, doch der verschwand nach seiner Amtszeit. Und mit ihm die archäologischen Fundstücke...

Because many of the villages surrounding Wiesenttal have Celtic names, the conclusion could be drawn that the place was populated by Celts about 2,500 years ago. Based on this insight, one might interpret the geometric formation of the mossy rocks which are strewn about here, as being a Celtic ritual site. The individual stones have names such as "Baptismal Fount," "Sacrificial Alter," and "Guardian Stone." The main stone at the entrance of Druids' Grove has an incline of 51.5 degrees, which, incidentally, is exactly the same as the incline of the Egyptian Pyramids; the number of rocks just happens to be equivalent to the number of days in the Celtic calendar.

Apparently, the Nazis, in their "Germanic research," even did some investigation here, attempting to redirect the cosmic energy of one of the stones towards their leader, Adolf Hitler. In response to this, handfuls of "wise" men and women continue to hang around the grove, healing the stones of their "bad energy influence" by resting their hands on them. There are also the odd sickly looking young people who, dressed in all black, like to mumble strange words here by candlelight.

What you do not find, is any sound proof that Druids were actually ever here. Nothing was found through excavation, and the stones have no markings or inscriptions. On top of that, geologists from the University of Erlangen have found that these particular rock formations are based on natural tectonic characteristics of the area.

One citizen of nearby Wohlmannsgesees told us though, that there was a real Druids' Grove, but at another location. When he was a young man, he had actually found a golden arm ring, among other ritual vessels. He promptly turned these objects in to the local policeman. The policeman, however, mysteriously disappeared after his retirement, and with him, the archeological findings...

Eine Stein-Heilerin
A Stone-Healer

Steine, die helfen sollen, Vergangenes zu bewältigen
Stones which are supposed to help in coming to terms with the past

Druidenhain
Wohlmannsgesees
91346 Wiesenttal
Fränkische Schweiz

Der Druidenhain ist etwa 0,5 km südwestlich vom Ortsteil Wohlmannsgesees

The Druids' Grove is situated about 0.5 km in southwest direction of the village of Wohlmannsgesees.

Wanderpfad zum Druidenhain
The little path leading to the Druids' Grove

Das Regenwasser, das sich hier sammelt, soll heilende Kräfte besitzen
The rain water which collects here is said to have healing powers

Die Nebelhöhle
The Cave of Fog

„Auf der Alb ist alles anders", heißt es. Gemeint ist die Schwäbische Alb, ein auf Kalkstein liegendes Hochplateau in Baden-Württemberg. Schon die Anfahrt auf die Alb ist spektakulär: Steil geht es hinauf, als gäbe es einen Berg zu erklimmen. Oben geht es flach bis leicht hügelig weiter, runter erst wieder am Ende der Alb. Sie ist wenig besiedelt und vor allem bei Alt-Hippies beliebt. Bodenständigen Personen kann hier folgendes passieren: die Erde bricht einfach weg. „Dolinen" werden solche überraschenden Löcher im Fachjargon genannt, sie sind dem porösen Kalkstein zu verdanken.
Dieser ist auch für die Fülle von Höhlen verantwortlich. Olgahöhle, Mordloch – fast jeder Ort hat seine eigene Höhle und Geschichte dazu. Eine davon ist die Nebelhöhle, die im Roman „Lichtenstein" von Wilhelm Hauff eine wichtige Rolle spielt: Sie dient dem Fürst von Württemberg als Unterschlupf. Das wirklich spannende an dieser Höhle ist aber, dass sie, obwohl als „Schauhöhle" kategorisiert, noch weitgehend „authentisch" ist. Es gibt keinen Lift, der den Besucher ins dunkle Feuchte bringt, die Treppen gilt es selbst herunterzusteigen. Dabei wird von Stufe zu Stufe die Luft kälter und klammer. Die Lampen, die hier den Weg weisen, stammen noch von anno 1930, in der Höhle selbst darf sich jeder ohne Führung fortbewegen, ein paar handbeschriebene Blechschilder benennen die verschiedenen Räume der Höhle. Nur im Eingangsbereich ertönt ein ausgeleiertes Tonband, um dem Besucher das Standardwissen zu Stalaktiten und Stalagniten zu erläutern.
Die Nebelhöhle ist genau so wie eine Höhle zu sein hat: ungefährlich und archaisch.

"On the Alb, everything is different." The speaker here was referring to the Swabian Alb, a high altitude mesa that lies on a mountain of limestone in Baden-Württemberg. The ride up to the top is spectacular. It is an extremely steep climb and you get the feeling you are scaling the face of a great mountain. Towards the top, it becomes hilly, and then flat, not going back downward until you reach the Alb's end, some 60 kilometers later. The limestone mesa is lightly populated and especially beloved by old hippies. More down-to-earth-type people may be in danger here, as the following can happen: you take a step, and the earth beneath you just falls away. The surprising holes that are left behind are called "Dolinen" in Alb-lingo, and are created thanks to the porous limestone.
This same is also responsible for the plethora of caves which are to be found here. Olga's Hollow, Murder's Pit – almost every town has its own cave, each one with its own story. One of these is Foggy Hollow, which played a very important role in Wilhelm Hauff's novel, Lichtenstein: It served as a hideout for the Duke of Württemberg. The real thrill about this cave however, is that though it is designated as a "show-cave," it is authentic to the utmost. There is no elevator to take visitors down into its depths, but only a set of limestone stairs with which to journey down into the darkness. The air becomes colder and damper with each step, and the lanterns that light the way date from about 1930. In the cave itself, you are completely free to move around as you please, without a guide. A couple of hand written signs serve to name each "room" of the cave. It is only at the entrance, that a tape recorder drones out the standard information about stalactites and stalagmites. Foggy Cave is exactly what a cave should be, not too dangerous, and wonderfully primitive.

Extra beleuchtet: Stalagniten und Stalaktiten
Specially lit: Stalactites and Stalagmites

Gemeinde Sonnenbühl
Hauptstraße 2
72820 Sonnenbühl

p: 07128. 925 18

www.sonnenbuehl.de/php/
nebelhoehle.php

Öffnungszeiten:
März und November Sa, So
und an Feiertagen:
9.00 – 17.00 Uhr
April bis Oktober täglich
9.00 – 17.30 Uhr

Opening hours:
March to November Sat, Sun
and holidays
9 am – 5 pm
April to October daily from
9 am – 5.30 pm

Eintrittspreise:
Erwachsene: 3 Euro
Kinder von 6 – 14 Jahre: 2 Euro
Familien: 8 Euro
Kinder bis 6 Jahre frei

Entrance Fee:
Adults: 3 Euros
Children age 6 – 14: 2 Euros
Families: 8 Euros
Children under age 6 are free.

Die Steine am Abend: gleich geht's hier ab
The stones at dusk: it's about to really go off here

Nächtliche Kraftsteine
Power Rocks at Night

Mitten im Teutoburger Wald erhebt sich unerwartet die bizarre Felsformation der Externsteine. Die Beschaffenheit der Steine lässt vermuten, dass sie einst ein Kultplatz gewesen sein müssen – doch belegt ist das weder durch Funde noch Ausgrabungen.
Tatsache ist, dass Karl der Große die Steine christlich weihen ließ und dass sich später die Nazis mächtig für die Steine interessierten. Sie ließen sogar das gesamte Gebiet um die Steine herum absperren. Die Nazis – vor allem um Himmler herum – spekulierten darauf, sich die dort vermuteten Naturkräfte zu eigen machen zu können. Eine fünfspurige Straße zeugt heute noch davon, wie umtriebig die Nazis hier geforscht haben müssen.
Heute wird diese Straße von Tourbussen und den vielen Besuchern genutzt. Täglich von 10 bis 18 Uhr kann man die Externsteine besuchen, sie beklettern, sich ein wenig mit der Natur verbunden fühlen und an alte Riten denken. Nach 18 Uhr allerdings wird der Wald um die Steine herum lebendig. Schamanen und solche, die es werden wollen, kommen aus dem Gestrüpp gekrochen und zelebrieren die Nacht hindurch mit Didgeridoos, Trommeln und Flöten, mit bewusstseinserweiternden Drogen und rituellen Tänzen. Man unterhält sich über Kugelschreiber, die von

Deep in the most German of all German forests, the Teutoburger Wald, a huge set of rock formations appears out of nowhere. Called the Extern Stones, the rocks' appearance suggests that they might have once been a Pagan ritual site. So far however, nothing has been dug up which has been able to prove this.
What we do know, is that Charles the Great had the Extern Stones christened, and that the Nazis seemed to have had a very strong interest in these rocks. The Nazis had closed the entire area off, and proceeded to make investigations into how to harness the spiritual power of the stones. A 5-lane highway stands to show us just how interested they were.
Today, this highway is mainly used by thousands of tourists who come here each year, packed into tour busses. They come to climb the stones, which are open for this activity between 10 a.m. and 6 p.m. This is a great place to get in touch with the surrounding nature, or to imagine ancient rituals taking place.
The real fun, however, starts at 6 p.m. after the park closes. Once the tourists have left, a couple of shamen, and other spiritually interested types, come out of the forest to meet at the rocks, where they celebrate throughout the night.

Das kleine Fenster gehört zu einer Felshöhle, in der meditiert wurde
The little window belongs to a cave in the rock, where people used to meditate

Mit Hilfe von Treppen und Brücken sind die Steine „erklimmbar"
The stones are "climbable" with the help of stairs and bridges

selbst den Lottozettel ausfüllen, und über Chillums in Indien. Brenzlig wird es nur, wenn die Skinhead-Tourbusse anrücken und auch ein wenig Nature-Power abbekommen wollen.
Bis um 10 Uhr morgens ist der Spuk wieder vorbei und ein neuer Tag beginnt.

Didgerideroos, drums, and flutes are played. Wild dances are performed, and psychedelic drugs are shared. Inspired by the stones, revelers like to discuss spiritual topics. Conversations about ballpoint pens which fill out lottery tickets by themselves, and about chillums in India are common. Some of these nightly visitors have been living in the forest around the Extern Stones for many years and appear here every night. Only the occasional busload of skinheads disturbs this otherwise peaceful setting.
The party goes on all night long until 10 in the morning, when the tourist day begins again. In the nearby forest, the last exhausted shamen are just jumping into their sleeping bags.

Blick auf die Steine vom gegenüberliegenden Ufer
View of the stones from the shore opposite them

Das ist kein Grab, sondern eine Tankstelle: hier sollen Erdkraftlinien zusammenlaufen
That is no grave, but a fill-up station: Earth-energy-lines are supposed to cross each other here

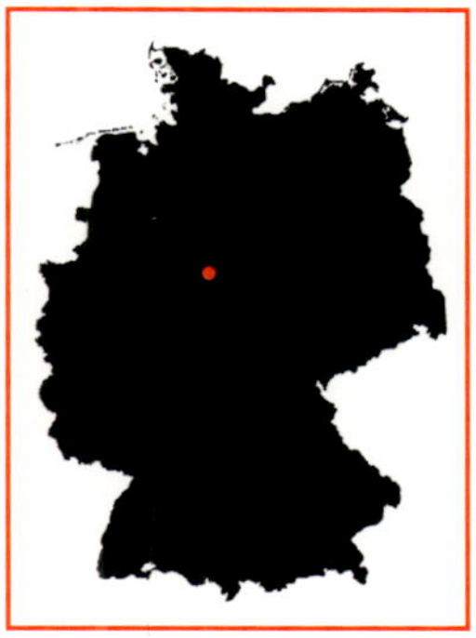

Die Externsteine
The Extern Stones
Forstamt Horn
Schmales Feld 21
32805 Horn-Bad Meinberg

p: 05234. 3200

f: 05234. 69386

www.landesverband-lippe.de

Die Steine am Morgen; bald kommen die Touristen
The stones at dawn; the tourists will be arriving shortly

Blauer geht's nicht

The Big Blue

Mystisch und unwirklich blau leuchtet es aus dem Inneren des kleinen Teiches „Blautopf" am Rande des idyllischen Örtchens Blaubeuren nahe der Schwäbischen Alb. Die extreme Klarheit des Wassers und die Tiefe des Teiches sollen die Ursache für die einzigartige Farblichkeit des Blautopfes sein – dennoch bleibt etwas Geheimnisvolles in dieser Farbe. Der Taucher und Hobbyforscher Jochen Hasenmeyer hat viele Jahre damit verbracht, dem Blautopf auf den Grund zu kommen: Er taucht immer wieder in ihn hinein und hat schon fast 18 km eines weitläufigen Höhlensystems erforschen können – und noch immer kein Ende in Sicht. Das wahre Geheimnis des Blautopfes hat noch keiner lösen können – auch nicht Hasenmeyer, denn der hat sich auf einer seiner Tauchtouren lebensgefährlich verletzt und kann ihn nicht weiter erforschen. Vielleicht gibt die Sage „die blaue Lau", die Eduard Mörike inspirierte, Aufschluss über das Geheimnis des Blautopfes. Der Sage nach war die schöne Wassernixe Lau mit einem Wassermann im Schwarzen Meer verheiratet. Da sie ihm keine Kinder gebären konnte, weinte sie ständig, so dass der Wassermann sie verbannte. Die unglückliche Lau schwamm lange durch Höhlen und unterirdische Flüsse, bis sie im Blautopf auftauchte. Hier beobachtete sie die Mönche und vorbeigehenden Besucher und das alles gefiel ihr so gut, dass sie bald wieder lachen konnte. Man munkelt, dass diese Sage einen wahren Kern hat: Wissenschaftler gehen davon aus, dass der Blautopf an das längste bekannte Höhlensystem Europas angeschlossen ist.

There is something strange about the little pond which is nestled at the edge of town in idyllic Blaubeuren, near the Swabian Alb. The color which emenates from its depths does not seem to come from this world. Called the "Blautopf," or "Blue Pot," because of its mystically radiating blue, the pond's extraordinary color is attributed to the cleanliness of its water and its amazing depth. Even this explanation, however, does not dispell the mystery surrounding it. Researcher Jochen Hasenmeyer spent many years trying to grasp the secret of the Blue Pot. Through numerous dives, he investigated more than 18 km of the cave system which is directly connected to the pond, finding no end in sight. The real secret of the "Blue Pot," however, has not been solved, and unfortunately, Hasenmeyer will never be able to solve it. While scuba-diving through the pond's underwater cave system, he had a life threatening accident, which forced him to abort any further attempts.

Perhaps the famous legend of Blue Lau, the water nymph said to be living there, can give us some clues as to how the pond acquired its supernatural-like hue…

According to the legend, the beautiful Lau was married to an Aquarius from the Black Sea. Because she was unable to give him any children, she was full of anguish and did nothing but cry – all day long. This was so annoying to the Aquarius, that he banished her from their home forever. The unhappy Lau swam for an endless distance through caves and subterraneous rivers, until she reached the Blue Pot. Here, she observed how well-natured the monks from the nearby monastery were, and noticed how the pond's visitors all seemed to be in good spirits. She was so pleased with her encounters that she was soon able to laugh again.

There could be some truth to this story. Researchers have formulated the theory that the Blautopf might be connected to the largest cave system in Europe.

Blick auf den leuchtenden Blautopf
View of the glowing "Blue Pot"

Der Blautopf
Aachgasse 7
89143 Blaubeuren

p: 07344. 921025

e: info@blaubeuren.de

www.blaubeuren.de

Schild am Blautopf
Sign at the "Blue Pot," which reads, "SWIMMING, DIVING, AND DRIVING IS FORBIDDEN!"

59

Speis und Trank
Meat and Drink

Thüringer Nationalgericht
Thuringia's National Dish

Das Nationalgericht der Thüringer sind Kartoffelklöße, am besten kindskopfgroß. Jeder Ort in Thüringen schwört auf sein eigenes Originalrezept, jede Hausfrau auf das ihre. So gibt es angeblich 18 972 Rezepte für Thüringer Klöße.
Auch zu DDR-Zeiten wurden die Klöße geformt und zwar planwirtschaftlich. Die ZBE (Zwischenbetriebliche Einrichtung) Heichelheim eröffnete 1968 die erste Kloßmanufaktur Thüringens und ließ die Hausfrauen aufatmen: kein Reiben und Pressen mehr, ab jetzt gab es Kloßmasse für die Genossen. Sie war so beliebt, dass sie bald zur Bückware wurde.
Seit 1999 befindet sich in der ehemaligen Produktionsstätte ein Kloßmuseum, das nicht nur über die Klöße, sondern auch über die Kartoffel selbst Auskunft gibt. Unglaublich mit welchen Fakten hier aufgewartet wird. Nichts anderes als die Kulturgeschichte der Kartoffel ist hier aufgearbeitet worden. Der Besucher lernt einiges über die Kartoffelblüte in Marie-Antoinettes Haar, von den Kartoffeln als Geschenk an einen kranken Papst und vom wahren Ruhm der Kartoffel: ohne ihre Einführung hätte in Europa die industrielle Revolution nie stattgefunden. Ihr alleine ist es zu verdanken, dass ein einzelner Bauer zehn Menschen ernähren konnte.
Wer nach dem Besuch Hunger auf Kartoffelklöße bekommt, fahre nach Mechelroda. Hier gibt es noch die echten kindskopfgroßen. Aber nicht in den Topf schauen und die Klöße nachzählen. Warum? Am besten selbst fragen.

Thuringia's national dish is the Kartoffel Klöße, or potato dumpling, and, preferably, is served having about the size of a child's head. Every town in Thüringen swears on the authenticity of its own original recipe, every housewife on that of her own. It is no surprise then, that there are 18,972 recorded recipes for the dumpling.
Klöße were also formed back in the former East German GDR, and there for the first time, under planned production methods. The ZBE (Zwischenbetriebliche Einrichtung, or roughly: Inter-production Facility) opened Thuringia's first Klöße manufacture in Heichelheim in 1968, allowing the women of Thüringen to take a huge sigh of relief: no more grating and pressing. Finally, there was dumpling dough for the comrades. These were so adored, that they soon became one of the most prized possessions of any household which was lucky enough to acquire them. The Klöße were so popular, that they were often kept hidden under the counter and only sold when asked for.
Since 1999, the once booming factory houses a Kloß museum, providing a wealth of information, not only about Klöße, but about the potato itself as well. The plethora of facts to be awaited here, is truly amazing. None other than the cultural history of the potato is presented here. The visitor learns of the potato flower in Marie-Antoinette's hair, of the gift of potatoes to a sickly pope, and of the incredible renown of the potato: without its introduction into society, Europe would never have withstood the industrial revolution. It is thanks to the potato, that one farmer alone could feed ten people.
Whoever might notice an appetite after visiting the museum should take the short trip to nearby Mechelroda. There, the original child's head size can still be found. Just make sure not to look into the pot, counting the number of Klöße. Why not? You had better asked the cook.

Die Köchin im „Einhorn" zu Mechelroda…
The Chef at the "Einhorn" in Mechelroda…

… und ihre kindskopfgroßen Klöße
… and her child's head sized potato dumplings

Kloßmuseum
Dumpling Musum
Im Dorf 1
99439 Heichelheim

p: 03643. 900015

e: klossmuseum@t-online.de

www.klossmuseum.de

Öffnungszeiten:
April bis Oktober:
Di bis So
11.00 – 16.00 Uhr
November bis März:
Di bis Fr
11.00 – 16.00 Uhr
Und nach Vereinbarung

Opening hours:
April to October:
Tue to Sun
11 am – 4 pm
November to March:
Tue to Fri
11 am – 4 pm
Or with appointment

Zen oder die Kunst der Imbissbude

Zen and the Art of the Sausage Stand

Bochum Wattenscheid – tiefster Ruhrpott: wer Hunger hat, geht zum ehemaligen Dreisternekoch Raimund Ostendorp in den „Profigrill". Nix mit Feinschmeckerkost: Hier gibt es Schnitzel mit Kartoffelsalat, Schaschlik, Pommes mit Jägersoße, Linseneintopf und Frikadellen. Ostendorp hat keine Lust mehr auf Haute-Cuisine: „Was hab ich davon, wenn ein Yuppie gelangweilt die Rechnung bezahlt?" Er kocht lieber „Hausmannskost" im Schnell-Imbiss und macht sein Stammpublikum glücklich.

Die Putzfrau brachte ihm die Bedienung der Friteuse bei, aber auch die anderen Dinge mussten dazugelernt werden: Im „Profigrill" schmecken die Gerichte so wie erwartet. Das Schaschlik wird mit einem Fertigschaschlikgewürz angerichtet, die Jägersoße muss schön dick sein, Veggieburger will hier keiner essen.

Die Gäste sind buntgemischt vom Krupp Vorstandsmitglied zur zugezogenen DJane aus Leipzig. Ostendorp kommt mit allen ins Gespräch und tratscht mehr als der örtliche Friseur. Es sind die kleinen Dinge, die das Besondere am „Profigrill" ausmachen: statt Pappteller gibt es Porzellan, das Bier ist hier etwas teurer als in der Kneipe nebenan. Das hält das trinkende Publikum fern.

Bochum Wattenscheid – deep in Germany's most industrial region: whoever is feeling hungry makes a stop at the once three star Chef Raimund Ostendorp's food stand, Profi Grill (Profi as in pro). Forget delicacies. Here on the menu: Schnitzel with potato salad, shish kebabs, french fries with Jaeger sauce, lentil soup, and good old meatballs. Mr. Ostendorp has had it with fine dining. "What do I get out of it, when some yuppie, bored to death, pays his bill?" asks Ostendorp. He prefers cooking "handy-man food" in his fast food stand, making his regular guests happy.

The cleaning lady trained him how to use the deep fryer, but this did not suffice. The three-star chef had a good deal of learning to do: The shish kebab has to be dressed in a premade spice mix, the Jaeger sauce must be nice and thick, and no one wants to eat veggie-burgers here anyways. At Profi Grill, the entrees taste just as they are expected to.

The clientele is mixed, spanning from office managers, to factory workers, to the lone DJane from Leipzig. Mr. Ostendorp gets to talking with all of his guests, and knows more gossip than the town's barber. It is actually the small things which make Profi Grill so special. Instead of paper plates, there are porcelain ones. The beer is a little more expensive

Ostendorp und seine Imbissvielfalt
Ostendorp and his food stand diversity

Der „Profigrill" ist nicht mehr und nicht weniger als die Umsetzung des perfekten deutschen Imbisses.

than that from next door, which keeps the drinking public a bit further away.
The Profi Grill is nothing more and nothing less than the realization of the perfect German food stand.

Ein hungriger Gast
A hungry guest

Ostendorp grüßend vor seiner Tür: er kennt hier alle
Ostendorp waving in front of his door: He knows everybody here

ProfiGrill
Bochumer Straße 96
44866 Bochum-Wattenscheid

p: 02327. 82361

www.profi-grill.de

Öffnungszeiten:
Sieben Tage die Woche
11.00 – 22.00 Uhr

Opening hours:
Seven days a week
11 am – 10 pm

Die Schnapswanderung
The Spirit's Hike

Die erste Mühle auf dem Wanderweg
The first mill on the hike

16 Kilometer, neun Schnapsbrunnen und viel Auf und Ab. Das ist die Schnapswanderung auf dem Mühlenweg in Ottenhöfen im Schwarzwald. Der Weg führt den Wandersmann an acht Wassermühlen, einer Hammerschmiede und viel Schwarzwald-Idyllik vorbei.
Die Geschichte der Bühler-Mühle ist ganz bezeichnend für diese Gegend in Süddeutschland. Vor mehr als 100 Jahren erbaut, war diese Mühle auch Bauernhaus und Wohnhaus für die Familie Bühler. Die Bauern waren Selbstversorger und bauten auf ihren bergigen Äckern nur Roggen und Hafer an. Der Hafer wurde geschrotet und an das Vieh verfüttert, der Roggen wurde gemahlen und für Brot und andere Speisen verwendet. Nichts wurde auf dem Markt verkauft, man war autark. Und um richtig autark zu sein, brauchte man eben auch eine Mühle. Wasser, das vom Berg stürzte, gab es genug, und so haben viele Bauernhäuser im Schwarzwald ihre eigene Wassermühle.
In den 50er Jahren des 20. Jahrhundert fand das große Mühlensterben statt. Viele dieser wunderschönen Häuser verschwanden. Zum Glück hatten die Bauern in Ottenhöfen noch rechtzeitig die Einsicht, dass ihre Mühlen etwas Besonderes sind. In den 70er Jahren wurde hier der Mühlenrundweg etabliert. Da die meisten Bauern heute

16 kilometers, nine schnapps wells, and a lot of ups and downs: This is the famous Schnapswanderung, or Spirits Hike on the Mill Route through Ottenhöfen in the Black Forest. The route takes the wanderer past eight old water mills, by one old water powered hammer mill, and through plenty of nature.
The story of the Bühler Mill is nicely representative of many others from this area of southern Germany. Built more than 100 years ago, the mill was both farm and home to the Bühler family. Farmers of the time were self-sustainable, growing only rye and oat in their fields. The oat was given to the animals, and the rye was used for bread and other forms of nourishment; nothing was sold at the market. The mills were indispensable to the sustainment of this way of life. Luckily, in the Black Forest, there was plenty of water flowing from the mountains to power them (thus their multitude in the region).
In the 1950's, this lifestyle began to die out, and most of the mills disappeared. Fortunately, the farmers of Ottenhöfen recognized early that their mills were something special, and worth preserving. The Mühlenrundweg, or Route of Mills, was then established in the 1970's. As most of the farmers switched from growing grain to distilling their own spirits

So bleiben die Getränke auch ohne Kühlschrank kalt
This is how the drinks stay cold, even without a fridge

vor allem Obst anbauen und daraus Schnaps brennen, war schnell eine kleine Belohnung für den Wandersmann gefunden. An sogenannten Schnapsbrunnen kann sich der Wanderer selbst bedienen: Je nach Lust und Laune ergötzt man sich an selbstgebranntem Schnaps, Most und Apfelsaft aus eigener Produktion oder dem guten Tannenzäpfle-Bier. In eine kleine Sparbüchse müssen 60 Cent pro Getränk eingeworfen werden – schön, so viel Vertrauensvorschuss zu erhalten!

from various fruits of the region, a nice little reward was created for the steadfast and thirsty hiker, adding a bonus to the whole experience. Each mill created its own fountain of spirits, where wanderers can serve themselves. There is juice, cider, and freshly distilled schnapps, all homemade. If you are still thirsty, you might want to treat yourself to a bottle of the delicious Tannenzäpfle (Little Pinecone) beer. All that needs to be done is to drop 60 cents per drink into a little savings box – good that they are so trusting here!

Typischer Schwarzwald-Brunnen
Typical Black Forest spring well

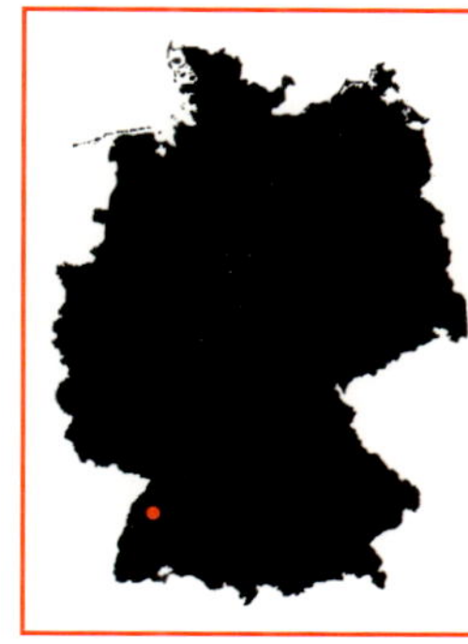

Touristeninformation
Tourist Information
77883 Ottenhöfen im Schwarzwald

p: 07842. 80444

f: 07842. 80445

www.ottenhoefen.de

Öffnungszeiten:
Mo bis Fr
9.00 – 12.00 und
14.30 – 16.30 Uhr
Sa und So
10.00 – 12.00 Uhr

Opening hours:
Mon to Fri
9 am – noon and
2.30 pm – 4.30 pm
Sat and Sun
10 am – noon

Peter's Grill
Hähnchen - Haxen - Würstchen

Monumente

Monuments

Mittelpunkt der Erde
The Center of the Earth

1932 erhielt der Bürgermeister des kleinen sächsischen Städtchens Pausa einen Brief von einem Professor aus Ägypten. Die Anfrage bezog sich auf einen metallenen Stein, von dem der Professor gelesen hatte: demnach befände sich im Keller des Rathauses zu Pausa ein Stück der Erdachse. Der Professor, der beim königlich ägyptischen Kultusministerium als Beauftragter für Metalle angestellt war, hatte schon den schwarzen Stein zu Mekka und andere berühmte Orte aufgesucht; in Pausa freute man sich über sein Interesse, denn die Geschichte vom Mittelpunkt der Erde war rein erfunden. Die genauen Einzelheiten weiß die Erdachsendeckelscharnierschmiernippelkommission e.V., die für das Schmieren der Erdachse zuständig ist, heute nicht mehr; nur dass es hier einmal zwei Marktplätze gegeben haben muss. Und wer sich hier verabredete, tat dies immer am sogenannten „Mittelpunkt", einem Kasten zwischen den zwei Märkten. Der Lokalpatriotismus des kleinen Städtchens und einige Beobachtungen machten daraus den „Mittelpunkt der Erde". Immerhin lag Pausa tatsächlich auf halber Strecke des Zeppelinflugs Nürnberg – Dresden. Irgendwann wurde der Mittelpunkt der Erde wichtiger als der Mittelpunkt des Marktplatzes und bald im Keller des Rathauses einquartiert. Hier ist er auch heute noch und kann samt zeremonieller Schmierung mit eigens dafür angefertigtem Likör erlebt werden. Denn, so die Erdachsendeckelscharnierschmiernippelkommission: Was für die Erdachse gut ist, muss auch für den Menschen gut sein.

In 1932, the Mayor of the small Saxon town of Pausa received a letter from an Egyptian professor. The inquiry was about a small metallic stone. According to the professor, a piece of the earth's axis could be found in the basement of Pausa's Rathaus (town hall). Commissioned by the Egyptian King's Ministry of Cult Phenomena as an expert in metallurgy, and having already done extensive research on the black stone of Mecca, the professor saw the metallic stone of Pausa as being the perfect new challenge. The town of Pausa was excited about his interest, especially because they knew that the story about the center of the earth had been completely fabricated.

Sadly, the details of the whole affair are no longer known by the Erdachsendeckelscharnierscmiernippelkommission, or the "Earth-Axis-Lid-Hinge-Oiling-Nipple-Commission." All that is known is that at one time, there must have been two market-squares in Pausa, and that whoever may have had a meeting with someone in Pausa did this in the so-called "middle point," a boxed area right between the two squares. Local patriotism in the little town, along with a little advice from outsiders, has turned this spot into the "Center of the Earth." As a matter of fact, Pausa does happen to lie right smack in the middle of the Nürnberg – Dresden Zeppelin route. Sometime along the way, the center of the earth became even more important than the middle point between the two market-squares and was moved down into the Rathaus basement. That is where it still is today, and is also where the ceremonial greasing of the axel, with the help of various lubricating liqueurs, can be wonderfully experienced. According to the Erdachsendeckelscharnierscmiernippelkommission, "Whatever is good for the earth's axel, must also be good for humans."

Erdachsendeckelscharnierschmiernippelkommission beim Schmieren
The Erdachsendeckelscharnierschmiernippelkommission, or "Earth-Axis-Lid-Hinge-Oiling-Nipple-Commission," doing an oiling

Rathaus Pausa
Town Hall of Pausa
07952 Pausa

e: erdachse@hahn-pausa.de

www.hahn-pausa.de/ ERDACHSE/Informationen/ informationen.html

Öffnungszeiten:
Mo bis Fr
9.00 – 16.00 Uhr
Sa, So und an Feiertagen
9.30 – 17.30 Uhr

Opening hours:
Mon to Fri
9 am – 4 pm
Sat, Sun, and holidays
9.30 am – 5.30 pm

Nähere Informationen erhalten Sie bei Frau Müller unter Tel. 037432. 60311

Please call Mrs. Müller for further information 037432. 60311

Sicht aus dem Turmfenster auf das Pferd von Kaiser Wilhelm
View of Emporer Wilhelm's horse from the tower window

Weißbart und Rotbart
Red Beard and White Beard

Als 1190 Friedrich I, der rotbärtige Barbarossa, auf dem dritten Kreuzzug einfach so in einem Fluss ertrank, wollte das keiner wahrhaben. Barbarossa verdiente einen heldenhafteren Tod. Er, der Deutschland vereinigt hatte!
So entstand die Sage, der Kaiser habe sich im Inneren des Kyffhäusergebirges zurückgezogen und warte dort auf den Tag, Deutschland aus dem Dunklen zu holen und in ein goldenes Zeitalter zu führen.
Der Deutsche Kriegerverein erinnerte sich nach der Schlacht gegen Napoleon (1871) dieser Sage: Man wollte dem siegreichen Wilhelm I, der Deutschland zum zweiten Mal geeint hatte, ein Denkmal setzen. Welcher Ort wäre dafür geeigneter gewesen, als auf dem Berge, in dem Barbarossa schlummert!
1896 wurde das Denkmal eingeweiht. Barbarossa sitzt da in rotem Sandstein gehauen, sich mit grimmiger Miene den Bart kämmend. Ein Soldat sei im 18. Jahrhundert zum Barbarossa in den Berg hinabgestiegen und berichtete, dass dessen Bart schon dreimal um das Tischbein gewachsen sei.
Über dem steinernen Barbarossa thront der kupferner Wilhelm I hoch zu Ross. 247 Stufen kann der Besucher erklimmen und hat eine sagenhafte Sicht (auch auf das

When Friedrich I, the red-bearded Barbarossa, simply drowned in a river during the third Crusade in 1190, nobody wanted to believe it. Barbarossa deserved a more heroic death. After all, he had unified Germany!
This is how the legend arose about the Emperor having retired into the core of the Kyffhäuser Mountains, waiting for the day when he would come back to bring Germany out of the darkness, leading the country through a golden age.
The German Kriegerverein (War Club) recollected thought of this story after the battle against Napoleon in 1871. They wanted to build a monument to the victorious Wilhelm I, who had now unified Germany for a second time. Which place could be better fitting than there in the mountains where Barbarossa lay slumbering?
The monument was consecrated in 1896. Chiseled from red sandstone, Barbarossa sits combing his beard with a menacing expression. A soldier is supposed to have climbed the mountains in the 19th century to visit the old Emperor. He then reported that Barbarossa's beard had grown so long that it had wrapped itself three times around the leg of his table.
Above the stony Barbarossa, a copper Wilhelm I is enthroned upon his royal horse. Two-hundred and forty-seven

Frontalansicht des Monuments
Frontal view of the monument

Säulen, mit mittelalterlich anmutender Verzierung
Columns with ornamentation remeniscent of the middle ages

Reiterdenkmal – genau dorthin, woher die vielen Pferdeäpfel kommen). Raben kreisen um den Denkmalsturm. Der Sage nach berichten diese dem Barbarossa in der Tiefe vom Stand der Dinge in Deutschland.

stairs lead up to the monument with its spectacular view (of, among other things, the Cavalry Monument – where all the horse dung is). Ravens circle around the monument's tower. As the legend has it, every now and then, the sharp-eyed birds report back down to the depths where Barabarossa waits, letting him know what the situation looks like in Germany.

Blick auf die Besucherplattform
View of the visitors platform

Barbarossa, sich grimmig den Bart streichend
Barbarossa grimly grooming his beard

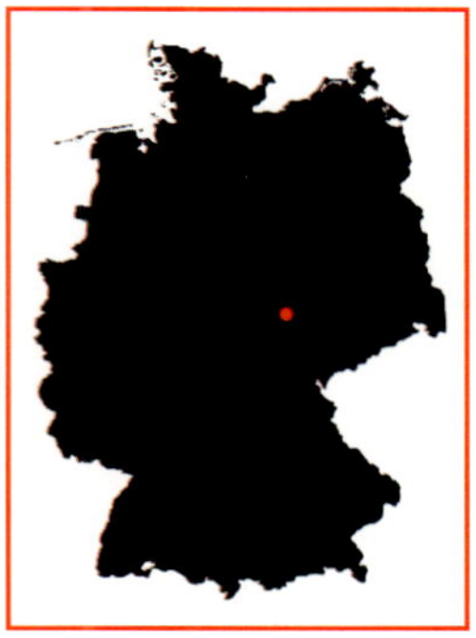

Kyffhäuser-Denkmal
Kyffhäuser Monument
06567 Bad Frankenhausen

Kyffhäuser Fremden-verkehrsverband e.V.
Tourist Information
Anger 14
06567 Bad Frankenhausen

p: 034671. 7170

Das Elefantenklo
The Elephant Toilet

Übersehen kann man das Panorama-Museum bei Bad Frankenhausen beim besten Willen nicht: Im Volksmund wird der Rundbau wegen seiner gigantischen Ausmaße gerne Elefantenklo genannt.

Am 14. September 1989, also kurz vor der Wende fertiggestellt, war das Panorama-Museum ursprünglich als Bauernkriegsdenkmal errichtet worden. Es steht auf dem Platz, auf dem 1525 der thüringische Bauernkrieg ausgetragen wurde. 450 Jahre später, also gerade noch zu Glanzzeiten der DDR, fühlte sich diese ganz nach der sozialistischen Erbtheorie als „Erfüllerin des Vermächtnisses der aufständischen Bauern", verpflichtet, dem Aufstand zu gedenken. Es ging hier um nichts geringeres als um die historische Legitimation der DDR. Die Planung des Denkmals begann. Umstritten noch die Frage, was drinnen zu sehen sein solle.

Werner Tübke, Rektor der Leipziger Hochschule für Grafik und Buchkunst, trat von seinem Posten zurück, um sich ganz dieser Aufgabe zu widmen und entwarf in zwölfjähriger Arbeit, was später das größte Gemälde der Welt werden sollte: das Epochenbild „Die Frühbürgerliche Revolution in Deutschland". 14 Meter hoch und 123 Meter lang, übersäht von mehr als 3000 Figuren, ist schon allein die Fabrikation der Leinwand eine Meisterleistung (vollbracht durch die Genossinnen im sowjetischen Textilkombinat von Sursk). Und für die Grundierung der Leinwand wurden Experten geladen, die nach geheimen Rezepten russischer Ikonen arbeiteten!

Als der Bau stand, blühte die DDR schon längst nicht mehr und sein Sinn war im Ideologienkuddelmuddel untergegangen. Ein zweiter Spitzname entstand: Faultier-Ranch. Dafür blüht heute rund um das Elefantenklo die Butterfahrten-Industrie.

No matter how hard you try, you cannot miss spotting the Panorama-Museum near Bad Frankenhausen. Known on the streets as the Elephant Toilet, it sticks out like a sore thumb. On the 14th of September 1989, just before the wall came down, construction was completed on the round building, which was conceived of as a monument to the peasants. It stands in the square where the Thuringian Peasants War of 1525 took place. Four hundred and fifty years later, the GDR was in its prime and, true to socialist ideology, seeing themselves as the "fulfillers of the legacy of the peasants revolt," the government felt obliged to commemorate the event. This endeavor was actually about nothing less than the historical legitimacy of the GDR. Planning for the memorial began. The only question was, what should the building house?

Werner Tübke, rector of the Leipziger Hochschule für Grafik und Buchkunst (Leipziger College of Graphic Design and Book Arts), stepped down from his post in order to devote himself fully to the project. He then spent twelve years working on what would become the biggest painting in the world: the epic painting, of the Early Citizens' Revolution in Germany. Adorned by more than 3,000 figures, fourteen meters high, and 123 meters long, the canvas itself is a work of art. Its production was achieved by comrades in the Soviet textile plant in Sursk, and the ground was applied by experts from Russia who worked using a secret ancient icon recipe!

When the project was finally finished, the GDR had already been in decline for some time, and the building's significance was drowned in a pool of ideological mush. A second nickname emerged: Lame-Beast Ranch. To make up for it, the tour-bus industry is now booming around the elephant toilet.

Die Innenseite der runden Wand wird vom größten Ölgemälde der Welt bedeckt
The interior of the round wall is covered with the biggest oil painting in the world

Panorama Museum
Am Schlachtberg 9
06567 Bad Frankenhausen

p: 034671. 6190
f: 034671. 61920
www.panorama-museum.de

Öffnungszeiten:
April bis September:
Di bis So 10.00 – 18.00 Uhr
Oktober bis März:
Di bis So 10.00 – 17.00 Uhr
In den Monaten Juli und August auch montags von 13 – 18 Uhr geöffnet.
Sonst ist das Museum montags (außer an gesetzlichen Feiertagen) sowie am 24. Dezember geschlossen.
Opening hours:
April to September:
Tue to Sun 10 am – 6 pm
October to March:
Tue to Sun 10 am – 5 pm
From July to August the Museum is also open on Mondays between 1 pm and 6 pm
Closed on mondays (unless public holiday) and December 24th
Eintrittspreise:
Erwachsene: 5 Euro
Ermäßigt: 4 Euro
Kinder: 1 Euro
Entrance Fee:
Adults: 5 Euros
Reduced: 4 Euros
Children: 1 Euro

Maria
bitte hilf mir. 1.Nov 93
hat geholfen

Der Feind von Anfang glaubt, in diesem dunklen Erdgewirre, Steh selbst der heiligen Bemühn dem Lügnertruge feil.
O daß dein Geist, o Christ, sich nie durch Schein geblendet irre, Sey dir der Glaube Licht, der Mühen Ziel das Seelenheil.

Wunderland Religion

Religious Wonderland

Ein Leben für die Weihnacht
Living for Christmas

Kevelaer ist das deutsche Mekka. Mit über 800 000 Pilgern jährlich ist diese Kleinstadt Deutschlands beliebtestes Pilgerziel. Eine kleines Marienbild in der Stadtkirche ist die Ursache für den Aufmarsch Tausender verzückter Großmütter. Und wo die Heilsuchenden hinkommen, da wird ihnen Heil angeboten: der Weg zur Kirche wird gesäumt von Läden für Kerzen, Bibeln, betende Hände und anderen Souvenirs.

Etwas abseits von dem Trubel findet sich ein weiteres Kleinod für die Pilgerer: Das HoDa Krippenmuseum (HoDa steht für Horst Dammers, das Familienoberhaupt der Krippenfamilie).

Laut Aussage der Betreiber gibt es hier „unzählige" Krippen aus der ganzen Welt ganzjährig zu bestaunen. Krippen mit mannshohen Figuren bis hin zu einer Krippe, die in einer Streichholzschachtel Platz findet. Selbst Krippen mit Schwarzen und Asiaten gibt es hier.

Das HoDa Krippenmuseum und die dazugehörige Krippen-Manufaktur sind das Lebenswerk von Horst Dammers und seiner Familie. Seit über 40 Jahren werden hier Figuren geschnitzt, gegossen und bemalt. Und nie wurde ein Fremder an diese Arbeit rangelassen, denn der könnte das

Kevelaer is the Mecca of Germany. With over 800,000 pilgrims coming each year, this town turns out to be Germany's most popular place of pilgrimage. Masses of enraptured grandmothers march to the city every year in order to visit a small picture of the Virgin Mary in the local church. Where people seek for salvation, salvation is offered: The route to the church is lined with stores selling candles, bibles, praying hands, and other souvenirs.

Set apart from the main tumult, however, there is a somewhat quieter gem for the pilgrims to admire. The HoDa Nativity Museum (HoDa stands for Horst Dammers, the patriarch of the Nativity-family) houses "innumerable" nativity scenes from all over the world. There are life-sized nativities and nativity scenes which fit into a matchbox. There are nativities with Asian figures as well as figures of color.

The HoDa Nativity Museum and the related Nativity Workshop are the life works of Horst Dammers and his family. Together, they have been carving, casting, painting, and reworking nativity scenes for the last 40 years. Strangers have never been allowed to work along side them as the family's valuable knowledge and many secrets could be in danger of being stolen. Even husbands for Dammer's daughters

Im Krippenmuseum ist immer Weihnachten
It is always Christmas in the Nativity Museum

wertvolle Wissen der Dammers stehlen. Selbst Ehemänner für die Töchter wurden vom Patriachen nicht so richtig als notwendig erachtet: „Warum soll man wegen einem Glas Milch eine ganze Kuh kaufen?“ So haben also bis vor kurzem Vater, Mutter und die drei Töchter den Laden geschmissen. Und nun starb die Mutter. Ein Ölgemälde der „Mutti“ ziert seitdem den Ausstellungsraum und will den Besucher nicht so richtig in Weihnachtsstimmung kommen lassen. Die Atmosphäre der Halle, die stark an Industrie erinnert, ist dabei auch keine große Hilfe.

Nachtrag: Bei einem erneutem Anruf während der Produktion dieses Buches wurde uns mitgeteilt, dass Horst Dammers nun auch verstorben sei. Die Töchter werden aber Museum und Manufaktur weiterführen, so „wie es Vati und Mutti uns beigebracht haben“.

have been unwanted: “Why buy the entire cow when all you need is a glass of milk?” asks Dammer. Until recently, the business was run by Dammer, his wife, and their three daughters. Unfortunately, Mother Dammer passed away in 2002. Since then, a heavy oversized oil painting of Mother Dammer has dominated the exhibition room, keeping vigil and overseeing all who enter. This tended to make getting into the Christmas spirit a bit difficult.

Note: While working on this book, we learned that Horst Dammer has also passed away. However, the Dammer daughters are determined to continue the business, “just like Mom and Dad taught us to.” We wish them the best of luck.

Hier werden die Köpfe für Kaspar, einen der Heiligen Drei Könige, bemalt und getrocknet
The head of Casper, one of the three kings, is just being given the finishing touches here

Krippe in einer Streichholzschachtel
Nativity scene in a matchbox

HoDa Krippen Museum
HoDa Nativity Museum
Lindenstrasse 62
47623 Kevelaer

p: 02832. 7789

f: 02832. 404668

Öffnungszeiten:
Oktober bis Dezember:
täglich
13.00 – 17.00 Uhr
Januar bis September:
Sa, So, Di und Mi
13.00 – 17.00 Uhr

Opening hours:
October through December:
daily
1 pm – 5 pm
January through September:
Sat, Sun, Tue, Wed
1 pm – 5 pm

Die durchgelaufenen Schuhe
The Worn Out Shoes

In Bayern passieren noch Wunder! So auch im barocken Kloster Altenhohenau am Inn. Hier leben heute noch sechs Nonnen. Jeden Morgen findet sich eine Schwester, die die Puppe des Jesuskindes, die im Kirchenschiff auf einem Sockel steht, frisch einkleidet. Die Schwestern lieben ihr kleines Jesuskind, und im Winter bekommt die Puppe sogar wollene Unterhosen angezogen.

Die Puppe wurde einst von der Schwester Oberin Kolumba Weigl im 18. Jahrhundert ins Kloster gebracht. Damals war es üblich, dass Nonnen ihren eigenen Gegenstand zur Andacht mitbrachten – und die kleine Figur vom Jesuskind war bald von allen Nonnen so geliebt, dass sie anfingen, ihm die Kleider zu nähen und es einzukleiden.

Es wurde bemerkt, dass das barocke Schuhwerk des Jesuskindleins jeden Morgen aufs Neue ausgelatscht war. Man ließ die feinen Schuhe richten, doch es half nichts – jeden Morgen waren sie wieder zerlaufen. Erklären konnte sich das keine der guten Nonnen. Eines Nachts aber, als eine von ihnen noch lange ins Gebet vertieft in der Kirche kniete, hörte sie ein paar zarte Schritte. Sie drehte sich um und sah aus dem Augenwinkel heraus das Jesuskindchen durch die Kirche huschen. Sie folgte ihm und konnte beobachten, wie das Kindchen vor jeder Zelle der Nonnen halt machte und seinen Segen gab.

Die Nonnen von Altenhohenau sind heute alt. Sie blicken zurück auf ein Leben unter der Obhut eines munteren kleinen Aufpassers. Dieser steht heute noch in der Kirche in einer Vitrine; neben ihm seine zerlaufenen Schuhe.

In Bavaria, miracles are still happening. A perfect example of this can be found in the baroque convent, Altenhohenau. The convent is still active, though housing only six older nuns, all of whom share a very special responsibility. The Baby Jesus doll, which is exhibited in the nave, needs a regular change of clothes. The nuns are very fond of the doll, and in wintertime it even gets to be dressed in woolen underwear (it is cold in Bavaria).

The doll was first brought to Altenhohenau by the convent's most famous Mother Superior, Kolumba Weigl, in the 18th Century. It was then commonplace that nuns have a personal devotional object. Kolumba Weigl had her Baby Jesus doll, which she kept in her cell. The nuns found the doll so adorable that they began to sew clothes and shoes for it, changing its clothes on a regular basis. One day, while changing its clothes, the nuns realized that his shoes had become worn out – nobody could explain why. One night, one of the nuns could not sleep, and was walking through the convent. Suddenly, she saw the Baby Jesus doll. It was going from one cell to the other, blessing each of the nuns as they slept.

A little sign underneath the doorbell is also quite charming. It reads: After ringing the first time, please say the Lord's Prayer once, before ringing the second time!

Klingel an der Eingangstuer zum Kloster
The charming doorbell

Das Jesuskind
The baby Jesus doll

Dominikanerkloster
Altenhohenau
83556 Griesstätt

p: 08039. 903614

Die Nonnen beim Gebet
The nuns while praying

Wachsfigurenkabinett
Religious Waxworks

Tief im Herzen der Fränkischen Schweiz liegt der Wallfahrtsort Gößweinstein. Der Legende nach schon im Jahre 934 gegründet, doch erst nach dem Dreißigjährigen Krieg urkundlich erwähnt (Pest und Kriegsverlust trieben die Pilgerscharen hierher), zieht es heute immer noch jährlich an die 120 Wallfahrtsgruppen aus dem fränkischen Umland zur Basilika in Gößweinstein. Ziel der bis zu fünf Tage langen Wallfahrtsfußmärsche ist das Dreifaltigkeitsgnadenbild in der Basilika. Ihm werden Wunder zugesagt. Es sollte einst zum Bamberger Dom überführt werden, doch die Ochsen, die es dorthin ziehen sollten, weigerten sich, es aus Gößweinstein fortzubringen. Aufgrund der vielen Pilgerscharen wurde der Wallfahrtsort 1739 durch den Bau einer Basilika bereichert.

Viel spannender allerdings sind zwei kleine Räume zur Rechten des barocken Baus, im ehemaligen Messnergebäude: die Votivkammer. Sie ist gefüllt mit 75 Wachsfiguren, die seit 1860 als Votivgaben abgegeben wurden. Jedes Mal, wenn ein Wunder geschieht und ein Mensch von einer schweren Krankheit geheilt wird, wird hier eine Wachspuppe abgegeben. In hölzernen Vitrinen stehen aus Wachs gezogene Nachbildungen von Kindern, zwei erwachsenen Männern mit Schnauzbart und einer Frau in

Pilgrimage site Gößweinstein lies deeply hidden in the Franconian Swiss region of Germany. Though there are no written records of the place until the end of the Thirty Years War, according to legend, it was founded back in 934. In times past, pilgrims were driven to the church by the terrors of the plague and war. Though times may have changed, they are still coming here today. About 120 pilgrimage groups travel to Gößweinstein from the surrounding areas each year, the journey taking up to five days. They come especially to visit an image of the Holy Trinity in the church's basilica, which is said to have miraculous powers. At one time, the image was to be taken away to the cathedral in nearby Bamberg. This, however, was prevented when the oxen mysteriously refused to tow the wagon. The Trinity stayed. As pilgrimage increased over the years, the need for space grew, and in 1739, Gößweinstein was enriched with a new and massive baroque basilica.

More interesting than the cathedral itself, are two small rooms outside, just next to the church. These rooms are now being used as the "votive chamber." This is where 75 wax figures are stored, all donated to the church by various members of the congregation. The figures were given as a sign of gratitude when prayers had been answered or when

Fatschenkinder und ein Bein aus Wachs
"Fatschenkinder" and a leg made of wax

Tracht. Viele „Fatschenkinder“ sind auch dabei: wächserne, eingewickelte Säuglinge, die von lange kinderlos gebliebenen Eltern aus Dankbarkeit abgegeben wurden. Dann noch ein paar aus Wachs geformte Gliedmaßen, die geheilt wurden und Rosenkränze von Kriegsheimkehrern. Die letzte Votivgabe wurde 1952 abgegeben. Der damals zweijährige Heiner litt an einer Blutvergiftung mit Gasbrand. Das Bamberger Krankenhaus hatte ihn schon aufgegeben, doch die Großmutter versprach, bei Heilung eine Votivgabe zu stiften. Das Wunder geschah und Heiner lebt heute noch. Regelmäßig besucht er die Basilika und seine Wachspuppe.

sicknesses had been healed. There are replicas of children, full-grown men, and of a lady, on display in wooden showcases. Along with these are models of Fatschenkinder, or wrapped baby dolls, which were donated by parents who had been long without child.
If this is not enough, there are also a number of body parts to admire, all of which have been painstakingly modeled out of wax. The latest donation is the likeness of a small boy named Heiner. This was donated in 1952. The two-year-old Heiner had been suffering from heavy blood poisoning. The doctors in the local hospital had given up on him. Heiner's Grandmother then pledged to donate a wax figure, in the event that he was healed. The miracle happened, and Heiner is still alive, going regularly to church at Gößweinstein for a prayer, and for a short stop by his doll.

Wachspuppen von Menschen, denen geholfen wurde
Wax figures of people who were cured or otherwise helped

Die meisten Wachspuppen wurden in Bamberg angefertigt
Most of the wax dolls were sculpted in Bamberg

Basilika Gößweinstein
Balthasar-Neumann-Str. 2
91327 Gößweinstein

p: 09242. 264

Heiliges Öl
Holy Oil

Jedes Jahr zwischen Weihnachten und dem 27. Februar haben die Benediktinernonnen von St. Walburga im bayrischen Eichstätt alle Hände voll zu tun: aus dem Sarg der heiligen Walburga fließt das heilende Walburgaöl und das muss in goldenen Schalen aufgefangen werden. Wie oft und in welchen Variationen es schon leidenden und kranken Menschen geholfen hat, davon zeugen die vielen Votivtafeln im Kirchenschiff von St. Walburga. Aber auch Krücken, Zähne und sogar Nierensteine haben ein Plätzchen gefunden. Bald wird hier kein Winkel mehr frei sein, denn immer noch kommen Menschen aus der ganzen Welt hierher gepilgert, um für ein Fläschchen Öl zu bitten. Heute leben hier 55 Nonnen, nichts hat sie von ihrem Glauben abbringen können – wie eine alte Nonne mit typisch benediktinerischer Halskrause erzählt: Nicht die Pest, nicht der Dreißigjährige Krieg und selbst die Nationalsozialisten konnten die Glaubensgemeinschaft nicht ausrotten. Seit den 30er Jahren des 20. Jahrhunderts gibt es sogar Walburga-Ableger in den USA.

Die Heilige Walburga ist eine Frau mit spannender Biografie. Sie ist nicht nur die hilfeleistende Nonne, sondern auch die Namensgeberin der heidnischen Walpurgisnacht. Ihr Onkel ist kein geringerer als der Heilige Bonifatius, der „Apostel der Deutschen". Walburga, die um 710 in ein englisches Adelsgeschlecht geboren wurde, zog als junge Frau zusammen mit ihren Brüdern Wunnibald und Winnibald ins Land der Germanen. Im Kloster Heidenheim nahm sie das Amt der Äbtissin an. Vielleicht stammt die Verbindung zur Walpurgisnacht aus dieser Zeit, denn das Kloster Heiden(!)heim war ein Doppelkloster für Männer und Frauen, in dem nach angelsächsischer Tradition die heidnischern Gebräuche noch lange erhalten wurden.

Obwohl heute der 27. Februar als Todestag der Walburga gilt, wird vermutet, dass er am 1. Mai (die Nacht des Hexentanzes) war. Um sich ein Fläschchen Öl zu kaufen, einfach bei den Nonnen anfragen.

Every year between Christmas and the 27th of February, the Benedictine nuns from St. Walburga in the Bavarian Eichstätt have got their hands full: They are busy tapping a healing oil which flows from the holy St. Walburga's coffin, collecting it in golden chalices. The votive boards in the nave of St. Walburga testify to the many ways in which this oil has healed the sick and the suffering. Soon there will not be any room left amongst the crutches, teeth, and even kidney stones, which, in gratitude, have also found their way into the nave. People continue to travel from all around the world in pilgrimage to the church, just to get hold of a small bottle of the precious oil. Today, fifty-five nuns are living at St. Walburga, and there is nothing that can tear them away. An old nun, wearing the typical Benedictine habit, with its high embroidered collar, explains: "Not the black plague, not the Thirty Years War, and not even the Nazis were able to uproot this sturdy community of faith."
The holy St. Walburga is a woman with an incredible biography. She was an exceptionally active and benevolent nun, doing much for charity and for the world around her. She also happens to be the namesake of the pagan celebration, Walpurgisnacht, the night of the first of May when witches fly down to meet the Devil for a wild dance. Her uncle was none other than the holy Boniface, the "apostle of the Germans." Walburga, born of the English nobility in 710, moved as a young lady together with her brothers, Winnibald and Wunnibald, to the land of the Germans. There, she took office as Abbess in the cloister Heidenheim. It may be that the connection to Walpurgisnacht comes from this time period. Heidenheim (which literally means home of the Pagans) was a double cloister for both men and women in which, according to Anglo-Saxon tradition, pagan customs were long preserved. Although Walburga's date of death is said to be the 27th of February, it is suspected that it may have actually been on the first of May (the night of the witches' dance).Those interested in purchasing a bottle of oil can just ask one of the nuns.

Votivtafeln aus den letzten 30 Jahren
Votive boards from the past 30 years

Pfarrei St. Walburga
Walburgiberg 2
85072 Eichstätt

p: 08421. 1680

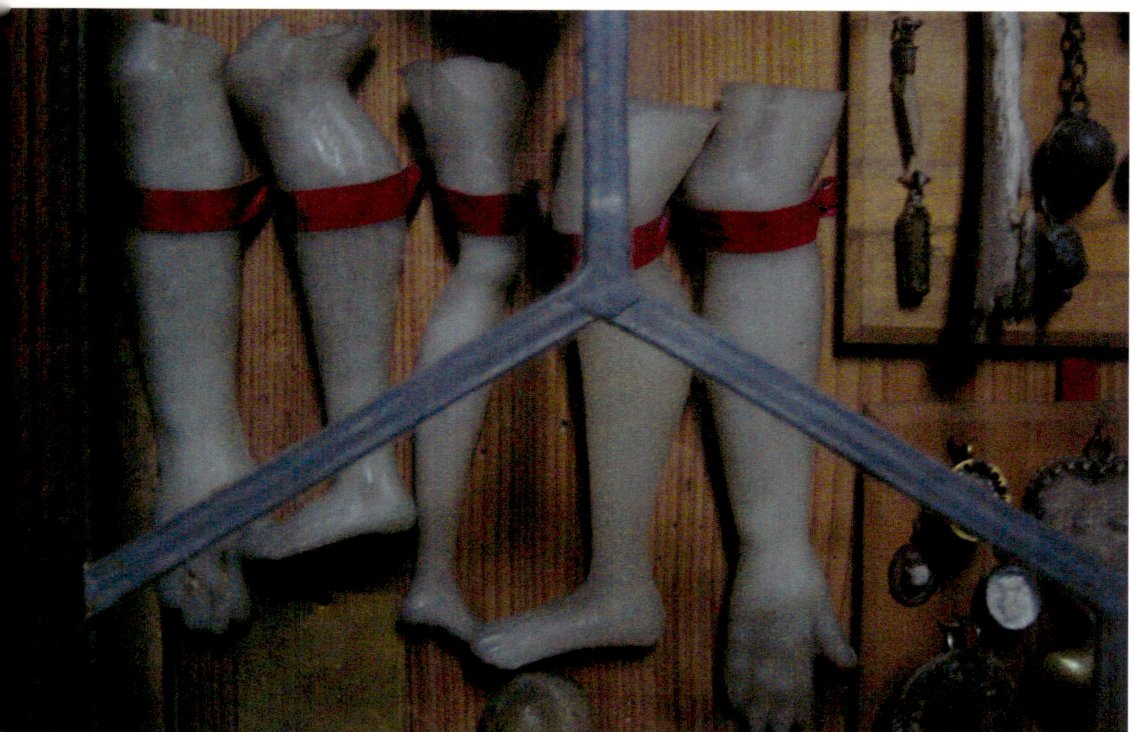

Aus Dankbarkeit aufgestellte Wachsglieder und Knochen
Wax limbs and bones which were donated in gratitude

Der fruchtbare Teigstein
The Fertile Dough-Stone

Nähert man sich der Kirche St. Wolfgang, spürt man die Jahrhunderte schlummern. Die Bäume, die Steine – alles scheint aus einer anderen Zeit zu stammen.
Tatsache ist, dass die kleine Wallfahrtskirche schon im zehnten Jahrhundert hier stand – seither wurde sie einige Male neu auf- und umgebaut. Die Wurzeln dieses heiligen Ortes gehen noch weiter zurück: Funde von versilberten Menschenschädeln deuten auf einen keltischen Kultplatz.
Die Kirche selbst wurde um einen Fels herumgebaut, der Fruchtbarkeit schenken soll. Dem Stein werden Kräfte nachgesagt, die das Christentum nicht ignorieren konnte, und so dichtete man die Legende vom Stein etwas um: Fortan ist es dem Heiligen Wolfgang zu verdanken, dass dieser Stein Fruchtbarkeit schenkt. Unter St. Wolfgangs feuriger Predigt sei der Stein geschmolzen – sei also zu einem Teigstein geworden. Dem Heiligen Wolfgang werden in Bayern mehrerer solcher „Teigsteine“ zugeschrieben.
Der Stein befindet sich vor dem Altar und ist mit einer marmornen Balustrade von drei Seiten umzäunt. Im Stein sind zwei knietiefe Löcher – die Fußabdrücke des Heiligen Wolfgangs. Der nach „Fruchtbarkeit Suchende“ setzt seine beiden Füße in die Löcher und kriecht dann durch ein Loch in der Umzäunung.
Der Rest der Kirche ist volkstümlich und schlicht eingerichtet – ein schöner Kontrast zu den sonst überladenen barocken Gotteshäusern der Umgebung. Einfache Bilder vom Leben des Heiligen Wolfgangs schmücken die Wände. Im Gästebuch bedanken sich viele Menschen.
Man sollte sich bei einem Besuch auch unbedingt mit der charmanten Messnerin unterhalten: Sie wird viel von den sonderbaren Erlebnissen in der Kirche zu erzählen wissen.

Approaching the lone standing church, you can feel the weight of centuries reposing on the earth. The trees, the stones – everything around St. Wolfgang seems to date from another time. The church was first built in the 10th century, but has since been rebuilt a few times. The roots of this holy spot, however, are much older. Findings of silver decorated skulls have suggested that this place was at one time used as a spiritual center by the Celts.
It is a stone at the center of the church which gives the place its special power. The rock is said to give fertility to those who ask for it. Dating back to the time of the Celts, this legend was later reinterpreted by Christians, in the story of St. Wolfgang. The stone is said to have begun to melt when St. Wolfgang stood on top of it to give a sermon. The saint's feet sank into the melting rock, and his footprints were etched into the stone forever, giving it the nickname "Teigstein," or "Dough-Stone." There are many such stones throughout Bavaria, which have been attributed to the fiery power of St. Wolfgang's sermons.
The stone is to be found in front of the altar, surrounded by three marble walls. In order to receive the full power of the stone, one has to stand in the saint's footprints, and from there, climb through a small hole in one of the three walls. This is not an easy task, especially for tall or weighty people, but according to the many entries in the church guest book, it is worth the trouble; the stone really does cure fertility problems.
The interior of the church is sparsely decorated, in relieving contrast to the many overloaded heavy baroque churches otherwise to be found throughout this region. The walls are adorned with paintings of the life of St. Wolfgang, which are pleasant and full of surprising details. We highly recommend speaking with the sexton, a very well natured person who knows many fascinating stories about the church.

Der Teigstein im Mittelpunkt der Kirche
The dough-stone in the middle of the church

Fremdenverkehrsamt
Tourist Office
St. Wolfgang Kirche
83352 Altenmarkt a. d. Alz

p: 08621. 984520

www.altenmarkt.de

Ein sehr fruchtbarer Hammel vor der Kirche
An exceptionally fertile male sheep in front of the church

Die Einsiedelei in der Stadt
The Downtown Hermitage

Böse Zungen behaupten, Väterchen Timofej sei gar keine 107 Jahre alt, sondern nur 104. So genau kann das heute keiner mehr nachprüfen. Tatsache ist, dass Väterchen Timofej zu Zeiten des Zaren in der Ukraine geboren wurde und nach langen Jahren der Flucht 1951 ohne Papiere in München ankam. Natascha, seine Frau, war bei ihm und gemeinsam bauten sie am Stadtrand von München eine russische Einsiedelei – komplett mit orthodoxer Kirche und Wohnhaus (heute Museum). Ihre Baumaterialien fanden die beiden in dem nahe liegenden Schuttberg, wo die Münchner nach dem Weltkrieg die Reste ihrer zerbombten Häuser hinbrachten. Natascha schmückte die Kirche innen liebevoll mit Aluminiumfolie, Blumengirlanden und Heiligenbildern auf Pappe und Väterchen Timofej pflanzte einen Garten mit vielen Obstbäumen und Rosenbüschen. Gemeinsam liebten sie es, mit vorbeistreunenden Münchnern zu plaudern.

Als man 1972 auf dem Gelände des ehemaligen Schuttberges die Olympiade abhalten wollte, sollte Timofejs Einsiedelei dem Stadion weichen. Zu diesem Zeitpunkt hatte das Paar unter den Münchnern so viele Freunde, dass sich die Stadt – vom Bürgermeister bis zur Abendzeitung – für die Einsiedler einsetzte: das geplante Stadion wurde einige 100 Meter weiter hinten gebaut.

So blieb Väterchen Timofejs Oase erhalten und weil München seit den 50er Jahren gewachsen ist, gehört seine „Ost-West Friedenskirche" mittlerweile fast zum Stadtkern. 1977 verstarb Natascha und wurde im Garten begraben.

Heute ist die Einsiedelei denkmalgeschützt und ein Russisch-Deutscher Freundeskreis kümmert sich um die Erhaltung des Gartens und der Gebäude.

Anm.: Zwei Wochen vor Redaktionsschluss dieses Buches verstarb Vater Timofej.

Some people claim that instead of being 107 years old, Father Timofej is only 104. This however cannot be proven. What is certain though, is that Father Timofej was born in the Ukraine in the time of the Czar, was on the run for many years, and arrived in Munich in 1951, without any papers. For this reason, it is difficult to establish his exact birth date. His wife Natasha had traveled with him, and together they decided to build a Russian hermitage, complete with Orthodox Church and house (where today a museum can be found), on the outskirts of Munich. The couple took most of their building materials from the nearby Schuttberg, or mountain of rubble, which is where the citizens of Munich had dumped the remains of bombed out buildings after the Second World War. Natasha decorated the interior of the church with tin foil, plastic flowers, and various icons. Father Timofej planted a garden with fruit trees and rose bushes. Together, they enjoyed making conversation with the passers by from Munich.

In 1972, when the Olympic stadium was to be built on top of the old Schuttberg, the decision was made to tear down Timofej's hermitage. By this time however, Timofej and Natasha had made so many friends in Munich that the whole city – from the Mayor to the local newspaper – campaigned against the demolition. In the end, Timofej's oasis was spared, and the stadium was moved back 100 meters.

As the city has so grown since the 1950's, Father Timofej's "East-West Peace Church" has become a part of what is now downtown Munich.

Natasha passed away in 1977 and was buried in the hermitage garden. Father Timofej, who was still in good shape, married a second time. The hermitage is now under monumental protection, and a Russian-German organization is taking care of the garden and buildings.

Note: Two weeks prior to the printing of this book Father Timofej passed away.

Ost-West-Friedenskirche im Olympiapark
East-West Peace church at the Olympiapark
80809 München

Hinter dem ehemaligen Olympia-Radstadion
Just behind the old Olympic cycling station.

Alles selbstgemacht: Die Alufolie an der Decke reflektiert das Kerzenlicht
Everything is hand crafted: tin foil on the roof reflects the light of the candles

Innenansicht eines Kirchenmodells
Inside view of a church model

Die Eitelkeit der Nonnen
Vanity of the Nuns

Die fränkische Sammlerin Maria Schwab nähte fast 100 Nonnenkostüme im Maßstab 1:12 nach. Genau so, wie sie vor dem Zweiten Vatikanischen Konzil von 1961 getragen wurden – denn davor hatte jeder Orden seine eigene Tracht. „Was weibliche Eitelkeit aus Schwarz und Weiß schaffen kann!“ Doch wie präsentieren? „Ich habe es zuerst mit Porzellanpuppen versucht, die sahen aber alle zu lieb aus. Dann habe ich die Puppen selbst aus Ton geformt. Jetzt sind sie wie die Nonnen, mal biestig, mal verschmitzt.“

Es finden sich auch andere Dinge aus dem Alltag der Schwestern wieder, so z.B. eine Besonderheit aus dem Orden der Birgittinerinnen. Dieser Orden, in dem meist Töchter aus feinem Hause aufgenommen wurden, bastelte kleine Figuren aus Pappe, kleideten sie in die Tracht der eleganten Birgittinerinnen und klebten als Kopf ein Foto der jungen Nonne drauf – das wurde dann an die Familie geschickt.

Außer den Nonnen sammelt Frau Schwab auch Devotionalien aller Art. Die meisten stammen aus Familiennachlässen. So ein Nachbau des Würzburger Doms aus Streichhölzern: Die Erben wollten das Riesengebilde nicht haben, aber wollten es auch nicht wegwerfen. Frau Schwab nahm den sakralen Bau in ihre Sammlung auf.

“Incredible, what female vanity can achieve with just black and white.” This insight inspired collector Maria Schwab to recreate nearly 100 nuns’ habits in the scale of 1:12, styling them just as they used to be before the papal council of 1961. Up until that time, each monastery had had its own unique dress code.

Eventually the question arose as to how to present the habits. “At first I worked with porcelain dolls, but they looked a bit too cute,” says Schwab. “So I started to make my own dolls out of clay. Now they look like real nuns, some of them beastly, others more mischievous.”

In her museum, one can find all sorts of other articles from the daily life of a nun. Among the collection there is a small handmade doll dressed in the elegant Birgittinerinnen habit. As it was forbidden to send pictures back home, nuns would cut these dolls out of cardboard, pasting a photo of their face onto the head, and dressing them in their order’s habit.

In addition to nuns’ apparel, Schwab collects various holy objects for use in the home. Most of the objects have been acquired through various unwanted inheritances. The family, for example, who inherited a copy of the Würzburg Cathedral – made of matches – did not know what to do

Handgemachte Nonnenfiguren: „Mal biestig, mal verschmitzt"
Handmade nuns: "some of them beastly, others more mischievous"

In Frau Schwabs Sammlung entdeckt man manches Objekt der Heiligenverehrung, das man bei exotischen Völkern vermutet hätte: Haarbilder, die aus den Haaren von Nonnen geflochten wurden, Plastikflaschen in Form von Maria – als Wallfahrtsmitbringsel, Totenkronen, Missionarsgegenstände. Und zu allem weiß Frau Schwab eine Geschichte zu erzählen.

with it. They certainly did not want to keep it. Not wanting to throw it away either, they thought of Maria Schwab. She was happy to take it. One might rather envision some of the objects in her collection having come from an exotic tribe from deep in the rainforest: pictures made of nuns' hair, a plastic bottle in the shape of the Virgin Mary filled with water from holy springs, and various missionary paraphernalia are among these. To each object, Maria Schwab has a story to tell.

Weihwasserbecken
Holy water containers

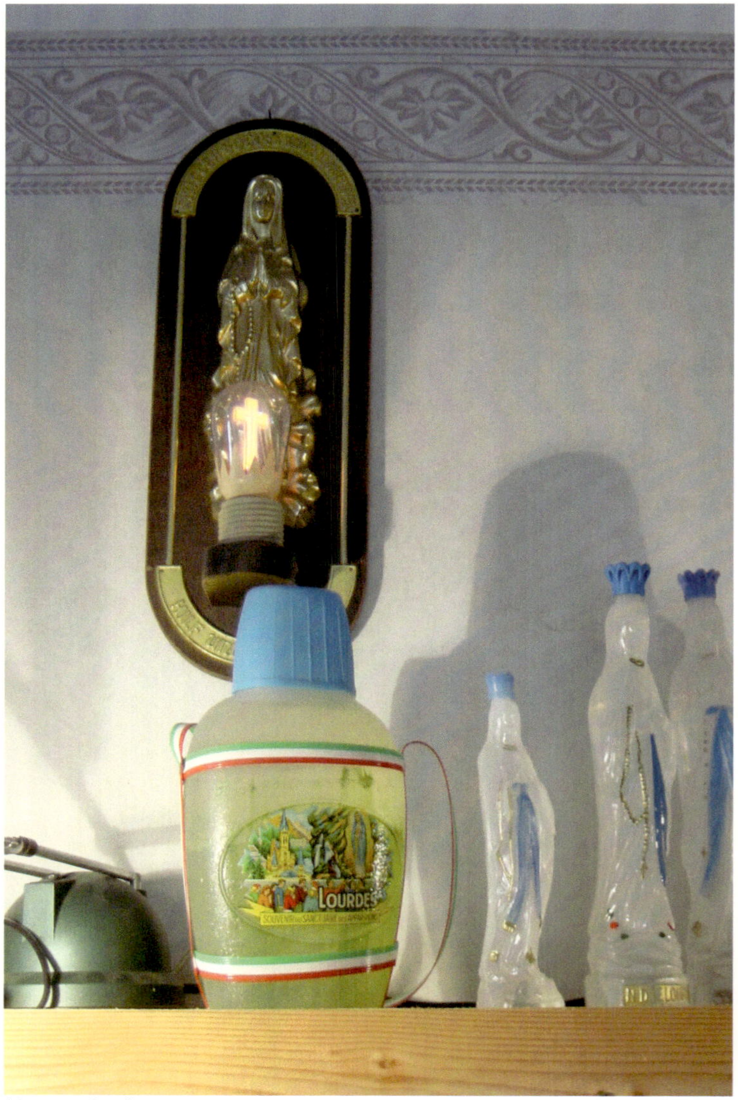

Marien aus Lourdes
Maries from Lourdes

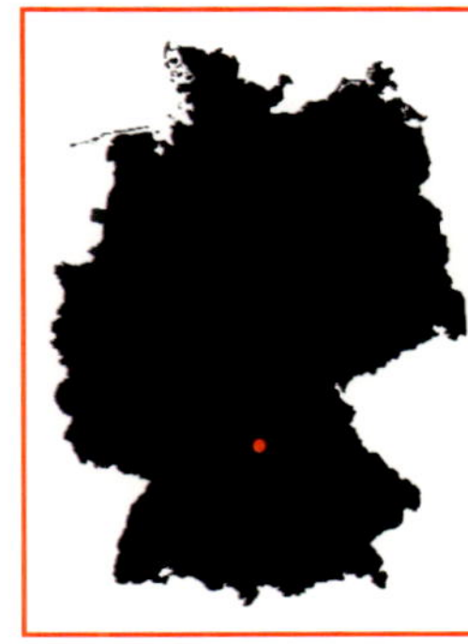

Museum „Klingelbeutel"
Otto-Menth-Strasse 11
97253 Rittershausen

p: 09337. 996889

Öffnungszeiten:
1. April bis 15. Oktober:
So 14.00 – 16.30 Uhr
Und nach Vereinbarung

Opening hours:
April 1st to October 15th:
Sun 2 pm – 4.30 pm
Or with appointment

Der Dom zu Würzburg: aus Streichhölzern
The Würzburg Dome: made of matches

Im Reich der Slawen
In the Land of the Slavs

Auch das ehrenwerte Fach der Archäologie ist den gängigen Ideologien untergeordnet. Während die Nazis vornehmlich Germanenkulte studierten, waren gerade diese zu DDR-Zeiten tabu. Slawen- und Wendenkulte, mit solchen Themen konnte man Forschungsgelder locker machen. Sehr erfolgreich war darin Professor Dr. Ewald Schuldt, der 1973 mit den Ausgrabungen am Sternberger See im heutigen Mecklenburg-Vorpommern begann. Hier vermutete er die Reste eines slawischen Heiligtums. Bis 1980 trug er über 90 000 Fundstücke zusammen, genug, um den Nachbau der ehemaligen Kultstätte zu beantragen. Und so wurde auf der Halbinsel am Binnensee bis kurz vor der Wende die dem Kriegsgott Radegast geweihte Slawenburg Palisade für Palisade wieder errichtet.

Die Festung ist ein wahres Mekka für Fantasy-Fans. Neben ihrem getreuen Nachbau reizt, dass sie nur zu Fuß erreicht werden kann. Jeder Schritt des 20-minütigen Spaziergangs durch den Wald, bringt den Besucher weiter in die Vergangenheit, bis zu den Toren des Tempels, zurück ins 9. und 10. Jahrhundert. Hier gibt es weder Würstchenbuden noch Souvenirläden, nur die schlichte Kasse katapultiert den Interessierten kurz ins 21. Jahrhundert. Flechtwand- und Blockhütten, ein Ringwall, Boote – alles kann betreten und

Even the honorable discipline of archeology is subject to bias under the common ideology of the time. While the Nazis promoted the study of Germanic culture, this same field was later taboo in the East German GDR. Slavs and Wenden Cults, on the other hand, were excellent themes with which to loosen the chains on the public funds box. A professor, Dr. Ewald Schuldt, who began excavating near the Sternburger Lake in Mecklenburg-Vorpommern in 1973, was especially successful in this endeavor. Here, he expected to find the remains of a Slavic sanctuary. By 1980, he had collected over 90,000 artifacts. This was enough to apply for the rebuilding of the once standing ritual site. The project was taken on, and until just before the change of government, the Slavic Temple Fortress in honour of Radegast, the Slavic god of war, was rebuilt, palisade for palisade, on a small peninsula on the lake.

The fortress is a veritable Mecca for fantasy fans. Especially enticing to the imagination, the incredibly true to life recreations can be reached only by foot. Every step on the 20-minute stroll through the woods takes you further and further into the past, until reaching the Gates of the Temple, which brings you back to the 9th and 10th centuries. Here, there are neither sausage stands nor souvenir stores. Only

Blick auf das Heiligtum
View of the sanctuary

angefasst werden, Hinweisschilder fehlen, das hier ist lebendige Archäologie. Mittendrin, auf einer Halbinsel im See thront Radegast, eine einfach geschnitzte Holzfigur, die starr aufs Festland blickt. Nur durch ein doppeltes Augenzwinkern kann man am anderen Ende des Sees ein paar Häuser entdecken – gäbe es die nicht, könnte man sich hier so richtig in der Vergangenheit verlieren.

the unostentatious ticket counter brings you back to the 21st century for a moment. There are walls woven out of wood, log cabins, a ring wall, and boats, all of which can be freely interacted with – a living archeology. In the middle of it all, sits Radegast, a simply cut wood figure staring out at the mainland, enthroned on his peninsula, surrounded by water. It is only when you squint with both of your eyes that you can make out a couple of houses on the shore across the lake – if it were not for these, you would really feel lost.

Der Gott Radegast
The god Radegast

Slawentempel Groß-Raden
Kastanienallee
19406 Sternberg/ Mecklenburg

p: 03847. 2252

f: 03847. 451624

http://212.77.232.153/~webfac/grossraden/_sites/offen.htm

Öffnungszeiten:
April bis Oktober:
10.00 – 17.30 Uhr
November bis März:
10.00 – 16.30 Uhr,
Mo geschlossen
24.12. und 31.12. geschlossen

Opening hours:
April to October:
10 am – 5.30 pm
November to March:
10 am – 4.30 pm
Closed on mondays
Dec 24th and Dec 31st closed

Das Haus eines Priesters
A priest's house

HUNDEBAR

Lerne für's Leben
Learning for Life

Doppelköpfiges Kalb
Double headed calf

Vom Zeitgeist vergessen
Forgotten by the Zeitgeist

Die kleine Stadt Waldenburg in Sachsen wartet mit ihrem „Naturalienkabinett" auf: Spannend an dieser Sammlung sind nicht nur die wild durcheinander gewürfelten Exponate, wie mehrere zweiköpfige Kälber, „heydnische Gottheiten aus dem antiken Ägypten", „Launen der Natur" oder 800 verschiedene Holzarten. Das eigentlich Faszinierende an dieser Sammlung ist, dass es sie noch gibt! Im Europa des 17. Jahrhunderts gab es mehrere hundert „Kuriositätensammlungen" oder „Naturalienkabinette", die als Vorgänger des heutigen Museums gelten. Im 18. und 19. Jahrhundert wurden diese jedoch fast vollkommen aufgelöst und gingen in andere Sammlungen über. So gibt es in Deutschland nur noch zwei dieser antiken Museen: eines in Halle und das in Waldenburg. Ganz sonderbar wird dem Besucher zumute, wenn er über die knarrenden Dielen schreitet, vorbei an mundgeblasenen Glasvitrinen, die penibel gefüllt sind mit dem Wissen der damaligen Zeit. Schuhe aus aller Welt stehen da gleich neben Riesenmagneten und Brennspiegeln, eine norwegische Schamanentrommel wird zusammen mit „aus Muscheln, sehr künstlich zusammengesetzten Tieren" präsentiert, auch Mumien und Schmetterlinge, sowie Kokosnüsse und Porzellanteller sind hier zu finden. Die vom Leipziger Apotheker Linck begonnene Sammlung

The small city of Waldenburg in Saxony hosts a very curious museum. Most notable about the Naturalienkabinett is not its collection of strangely strewn together artifacts, such as its double headed calves, its Heathen Gods of Ancient Egypt corner, or its Japanese shoes exhibit. Most notable about this place is its sheer existence.
In the 17th century, such "Naturalienkabinette," or "Curious Collections," existed all over Europe and have been generally accepted as the forerunners of the modern museum. In the 18th and 19th centuries, the collections were bought up by bigger museums, ceasing to exist. The collection in Waldenburg is one of only two such museums left in Germany, the other of which is in Halle.
The visitor steps into another world on entering the Naturalienkabinett of Waldenburg. The wooden floorboards creak as you walk by the meticulously arranged, mouth-blown glass showcases, which are filled with the knowledge of an earlier time. There is a collection of shoes from around the world, and of magnets and early electrical machines. There are Scandinavian drums, mummies, butterflies, coconuts, a collection of porcelain, and animals made of shells. The collection was put together by a Mr. Linck, a pharmacist from Leipzig, who then sold his life's work to the Count

Die Vitrinen aus dem 18 Jhd. mit Scheiben aus mundgeblasenem Glas
The display cases from the 18th century with mouth blown glass panes

wurde vom Fürsten von Schönburg-Waldenburg, ein weitsichtiger Mann, aufgekauft. Sein Anliegen: „Aufklärung und Intelligenz zu vermehren und Anregung für die Geschichte der Naturwissenschaften zu bieten."
Vom Zeitgeist vergessen, ist das Naturalienkabinett heute noch genauso erhalten wie damals und regt an, über die Haltbarkeit des Wissens nachzudenken.

of Schöneberg-Waldenburg. The Count's motivation in making the purchase was, "to spread enlightenment and intelligence, and to create an incentive for the people to acquire knowledge about history and science."
Forgotten by the Zeitgeist, the Naturalienkabinett looks the same today as it did 300 years ago, serving as an incentive to think about the durability of knowledge.

Physikalische und astronomische Geräte
Physical and astronomical instruments

Spirituspräparate
Spirited preparations

Heimatmuseum und
Naturalienkabinett
Geschwister Scholl Platz 1
08396 Waldenburg

p: 037608. 22519

f: 037608. 16060

e: museum-waldenburg@
t-online.de

www.waldenburg.de

Öffnungszeiten:
Di bis Fr
9.00 – 16.00 Uhr
Sa und So
9.30 – 17.00 Uhr
(in den Schulferien Sachsens
auch Mo 9.00 – 16.00 Uhr)

Opening hours:
Tue to Fri
9 am – 4 pm
Sat and Sun
9.30 am – 5 pm
(during school holidays in Saxony the museum is also open on Mondays from 9 am – 4 pm)

Blumentapeten, nicht nur für Blumenkinder
Flowered wallpaper, not only for flower power children

Tapetenwechsel
Wallpaper Scenarios

Von der Panoramatapete zur Fototapete, die kleinen Mietwohnungen Zugang zu karibischen Traumstränden ermöglichte, vergingen keine 200 Jahre. Was davor und dazwischen die Wände der guten Stube schmückte, zeigt das Tapetenmuseum in Kassel in einer einmaligen, über 18 000 Objekte umfassenden Sammlung.
Jede Tapete erzählt hier ihre eigene kleine Kulturgeschichte. So zum Beispiel die luxuriösen Goldledertapeten, die im Barock europäische Adelshäuser zierten. Sie kamen wegen ihrer langen Haltbarkeit in Mode und Bedrängnis. Denn, den Gesetzen des Zeitstils unterworfen, schien bald nichts langweiliger, als stets unter der Last derselben Tapete zu hausen. Goldledertapeten wurden von Seidentapeten aus Kanton abgelöst, später von Papiertapeten aus Frankreich.
Um 1800 entstanden die ersten Panoramatapeten, quasi die Vorläufer der Fototapete: nebst lieblichen Landschaften der Kontinente komplett mit Gebäuden, finden sich hier auch wuchtige Szenen, wie die Schlacht von Waterloo. Die monumentalen, teilweise auf 32 Rollen Papier aufgedruckten Tapeten fanden selbst in Australien Geschmack. Das Museum besitzt eine beeindruckende Sammlung von Biedermeier und Jugendstil bis zu Designertapeten. Wer bekommt hier nicht Lust auf einen Tapetenwechsel?

It took a mere 200 years for panoramic wall paper to develop into the photographic wall paper that we know today, having the power to turn a dinky little apartment room into a Caribbean paradise. Whatever may have covered the walls of German living rooms before and during this period, can be seen today in the Wallpaper Museum in Kassel, with its over 18,000 exhibits.
Every piece of wallpaper has its own special place in cultural history. Luxurious golden wall paper made of leather was cherished for a time by the baroque European Aristocracy. This wall paper became especially fashionable because of its extreme durability. Yet it was exactly this indestructibility which contributed to the paper's downfall. Such long lasting paper was unable to keep pace with the ever-changing modes of fashion, and eventually became terribly unpopular. These golden standards were then replaced with pure silk from China, and later with paper from France.
The first panoramic wallpaper was plastered up around 1800 and depicted anything from serene landscapes to Waterloo battle scenes. These monumental wall works used up to 32 rolls of paper and were popular even in far away Australia. The museum in Kassel hosts an impressive collection of these, followed by Biedermeier, Art Deco, and modern Designer wall paper. Thinking of redecorating?

So werden Tapeten gemacht
This is how wallpaper is made

Tapeten, in denen sich der Zeitgeist wiederspiegelt
Wallpaper which reflects the Zeitgeist

Deutsches Tapetenmuseum
Wallpaper Museum
Hessisches Landesmuseum
Brüder-Grimm-Platz 5
34117 Kassel

p: 0561. 7846141

f: 0561. 7846222

www.tapeten-institut.de

Öffnungszeiten:
Di bis So
10.00 – 17.00 Uhr
Mo geschlossen
24., 25. und 31.12. sowie am Tag vor Himmelfahrt geschlossen.

Opening hours:
Tue to Sun
10 am – 5 pm
Mon closed
Closed also on 24., 25 and 31. of December as well as the day before Ascension Day

Krankheiten am Mund
Diseases of the mouth

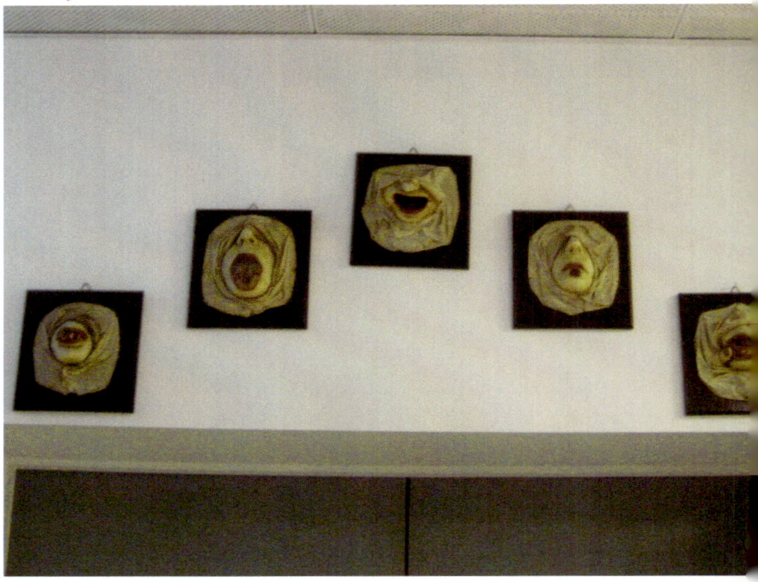

Heilige Apollonia
Holy Apollonia

Auch Zahnärzte haben eine Schutzheilige. Apollonia heißt die gute Frau. Wer sich die Sammlung im Museum für Zahnheilkunde in der Uniklinik Tübingen ansieht, wird auch bald verstehen warum. Hier sind zahnärztliche Werkzeuge aus den letzten 400 Jahren zu sehen. Eine Wurzelzange ist mit der Aufschrift „Vorsicht! Bei unsachgemäßem Gebrauch besteht Gefahr, den Kiefer mit heraus zu heben!" versehen. Apollonia kann also gar nicht genug gehuldigt werden.
Das Museum selbst ist kaum als solches zu erkennen. Es ist ein kleines, muffiges Zwischenzimmer und erinnert mehr an eine versteckte Gruselkammer, in der die Kabinetttüren besser geschlossen bleiben.
Einem der Autoren dieses Buches ist kurz nach Besuch des Museums ein Stück Zahn herausgebrochen. Er kann daher bestätigen, dass Zahnarztbesuche heute zwar immer noch kein Vergnügen sind, aber erträglich.
Die heilige Apollonia war übrigens eine frühe Christin aus Alexandria, die von Heiden gefangen genommen und gefoltert wurde: dabei wurden ihr alle Zähne herausgerissen und der Kiefer zertrümmert.

Even dentists have a patron Saint. She is known as St. Apollonia. Whoever might have the courage to go and visit the Museum of Dentistry in the University Hospital of Tübingen, will soon understand why a patron Saint for dentists is not necessarily such a bad idea. There are dentist tools that have been collected from over the last 400 years on display here. One Root Gripper is exhibited along side the following message: "Attention! If used incorrectly, this gripper can remove the entire jaw!" It seems that St. Apollonia can not be revered enough.
The museum is hardly recognizable as one. Rather small and badly aired, it is more like a chamber of horrors in which the chamber doors had better be kept closed.
One of the authors of this book lost a piece of one of his teeth shortly after leaving the museum. He can now confirm that visits to the dentist are still no fun, but are at least endurable.
St. Apollonia, by the way, was an early christian who lived in Alexandria and was captured and tortured by pagans. As part of her torture, her teeth were pulled out one by one and her jaw was smashed to pieces.

Verschiedene Goldzähne
Various gold teeth

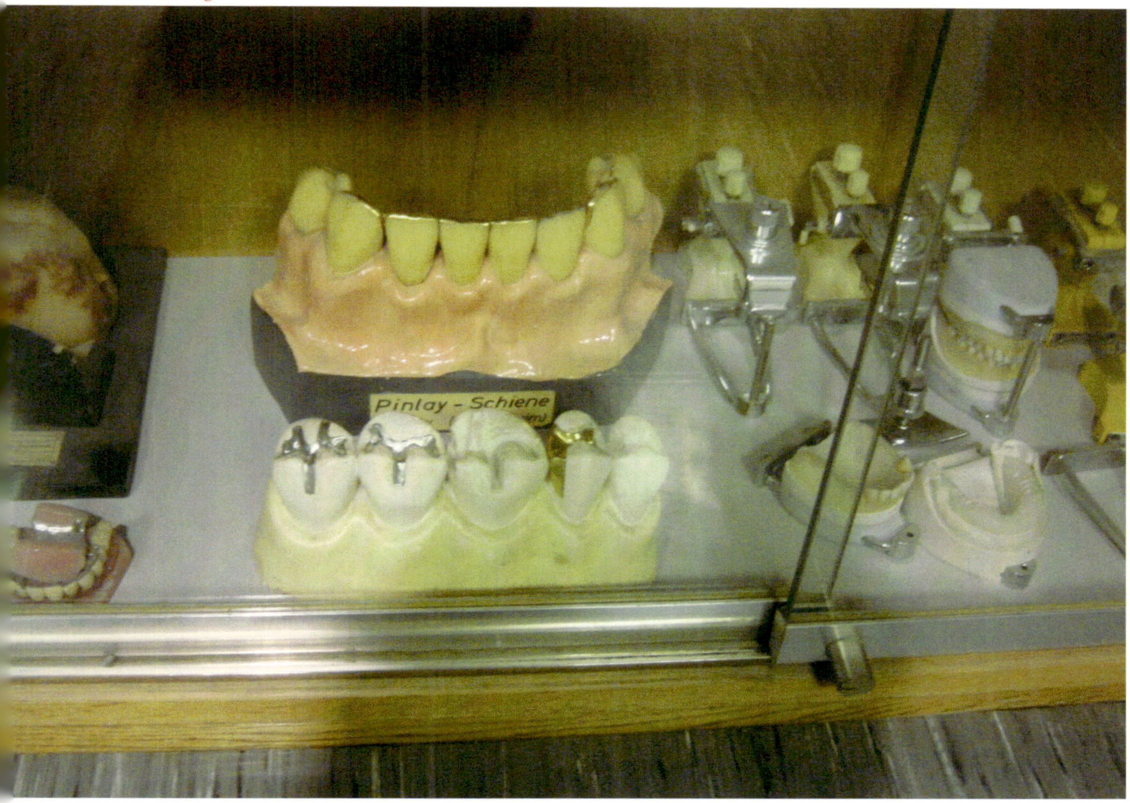

Museum der Zahnheilkunde im Zentrum für Zahn-, Mund- und Kieferheilkunde
Museum of Dentistry in the Center of Dentistry
Osianderstraße 2-8
72076 Tübingen

Das Museum wird betreut von Prof. Dr. Lindemann. Besichtigung nur nach Rücksprache:
p: 07071. 298 5180
e: drlukas@med.uni-tuebingen.de

Prof. Dr. Lindemann takes care of the museum. Visits must be arranged in advance phone or email:
p: 07071. 298 5180
e: drlukas@med.uni-tuebingen.de

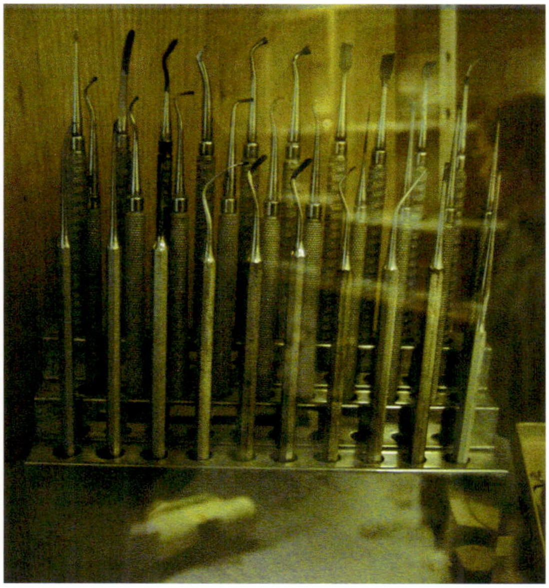

Werkzeug für Zahnärzte aus dem 18. Jahrhundert
Dentistry tools from the 18th century

Öffentlicher Geheimbund
Secret Society Gone Public

Dem Geheimen Bund der Freimaurer widmet sich ein gar nicht so geheimes Museum in der Wagnerstadt Bayreuth. In einer Gründerzeitvilla erhält der Neugierige einen Überblick über die Ritualgegenstände, die Geschichte und die humanistischen Werte der Logenbrüder. Wer sich mit dem Bibliothekar gut versteht, wird auch die ein oder andere Anekdote zu hören bekommen.
1933 plünderten die Nazis das Museum, das eine der umfangreichsten Bibliotheken über das Freimaurertum besaß. Das Logengeschirr wurde an Krankenhäuser und andere Institutionen, die sich nicht viel aus geheimen Symbolen auf Porzellanrändern machten, verteilt. Viele andere Schätze wurden eingeschmolzen und tauchten nie wieder auf. Lediglich die Abbildung eines Schurzes tauchte im Katalog der Nazi-Ausstellung „Entlarvte Freimaurerei" wieder auf.
Die Bibliothek wurde fast vollständig in Poznan, Polen, wiederentdeckt. Ein Vertrag über die wissenschaftliche Zusammenarbeit erlaubt es den Deutschen Freimaurern allerdings, wieder auf ihren Wissensschatz zurückzugreifen.
Eine ganze Sektion ist der internationalen Freimaurerei gewidmet. Während sich die Österreicher im Keller treffen, verabreden sich die Polen im „Hinteren Keller" (Deutsche Freimaurer haben keinen geheimen Ort). Es gibt bestimmte Phrasen und Kennzeichen, mit denen Freimaurer auch international kommunizieren können.

The secret confederacy of the Freemasons runs a not so secret museum in Bayreuth, the city where composer Richard Wagner came from. In a Wilhelmian style villa, interested visitors can gain insight into the rituals, history and even the humanistic values of the brotherhood of masons. A tip for those who would like to find out a bit more – it helps to talk to the librarian. He is full of anecdotes about the Freemasons.
The museum once owned the most complete library ever to deal with Freemasonry. Unfortunately, it was plundered by the Nazis in 1933. The Masons' tableware was then redistributed to hospitals and to other institutions who did not mind having to look at the strange symbols which adorned their new china. Many stolen treasures were melted down, most of the objects never appearing again. An apron emerged some time later, having been mentioned in a catalogue for the Nazi exhibition on "degenerate art."
The collection of over 80,000 books was rediscovered in Poland after the war. Thanks to a bilateral treaty on academic collaboration, German researchers now have the opportunity to use this library again. In the exhibition, an entire section is dedicated to the international aspect of Freemasonry: While Freemasons in Austria meet "fairly openly" in cellars, their brothers in Poland have to meet in total secrecy in the hidden backroom of somebody's basement. Do not miss learning a few of the cryptic phrases and hidden symbols that are used by Freemasons to identify each other all over the world.

Schild am Eingang des Freimaurermuseums
Sign at the entrance of the Freemasons Museum

Hammer und Logenschwert des Meisters
The Master's sword and hammers

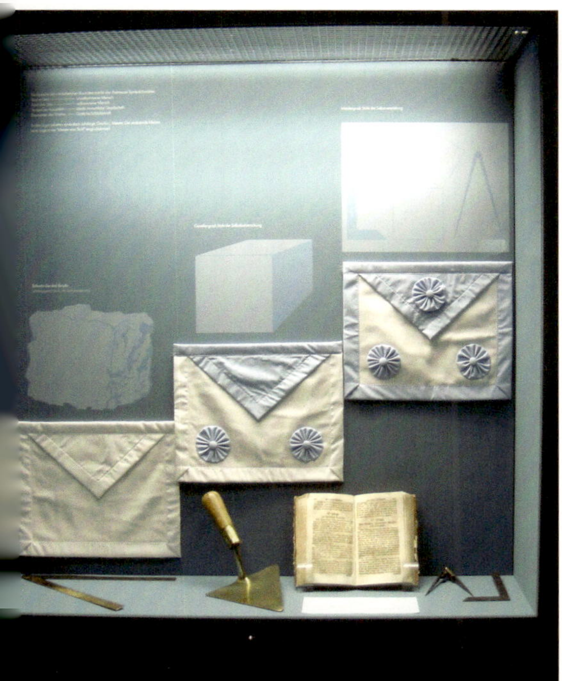

Schurze als Darstellung der verschiedenen Stufen der Freimaurerei
Aprons depicting the various levels of Freemasonry

Berlocke: von den Freimaurern als Schmuck z.B. an der Uhrenkette getragen
Medallions: worn for example by Freemasons as jewelry for watch chains

Deutsches Freimaurermuseum
German Freemason Museum
Im Hofgarten 1
95444 Bayreuth

p: 0921. 69824

f: 0921. 512850

e: deutsches-freimaurermuseum@t-online.de

www.freimaurer.org/museum/

Öffnungszeiten:
Di bis Fr
10.00 – 12.00 und
14.00 – 16.00 Uhr
Sa
10.00 – 12.00 Uhr

Opening hours:
Tue to Fri
10 am – noon and
2 pm – 4 pm
Sat
10 am – noon

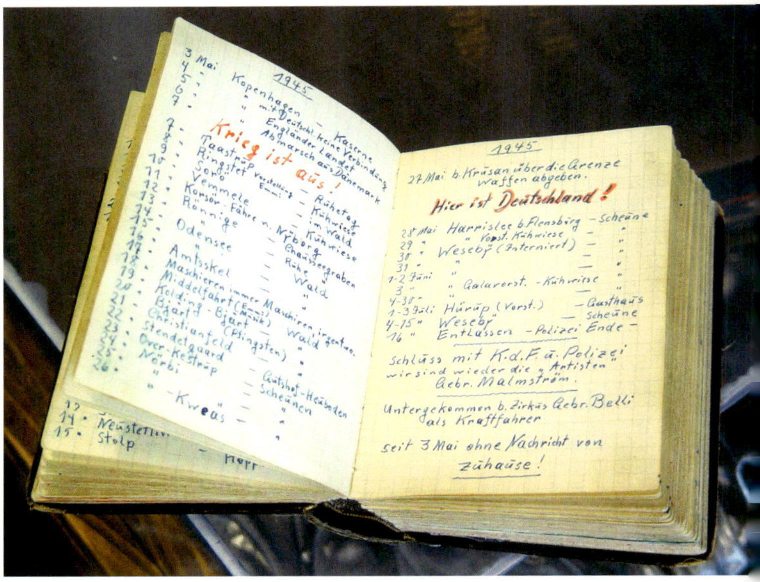

Das Fahrtenbuch von Großvater Malmström
The Malmström "bible"

Das Leben ist ein Zirkus
Life is a Circus

Groß ist die Zirkusfamilie Malmström und unendlich verzweigt. Jedes Mitglied dieser Artistenfamilie hat ein Abenteuer zu berichten. Und weils die Malmströms schon seit fast 300 Jahren gibt, gibt es der Abenteuer viele. Angefangen haben die Malmströms als Seiltanzgruppe. Ein Seil wurde am Kirchturm festgebunden, das andere Ende am Boden. Dem Urvater der Malmströms werden legendäre Fähigkeiten nachgesagt: Er soll über einen anderen Seiltänzer hinweg gesprungen sein!
Damit keine der Geschichten verloren geht, hat die Familie in ihrem Wohnhaus in Güstrow, wo sie seit 1917 beheimatet ist, ein Museum eingerichtet. Der Besucher wird von einem Malmströmer durch zwei Zimmer und einen Zirkuswagen geführt und bekommt zu jedem Gegenstand, der dort ausgestellt ist, eine Anekdote erzählt:
Von den Drei Malmströms, den besten Trapezkünstlern ihrer Zeit, bis sie herunterfielen und einer der drei, Hermann, alles doppelt sah. Von den Malmström Mädels, die in Amerika gastieren sollten, was die Mutter ihnen aber nicht erlaubte, da „die sich ja von so einem Öltycoon hätten wegheiraten lassen". Von der Malmströmbibel, dem Fahrtenbuch des Großvaters Malmström, mit dem Vermerk: „Hitler tot. Endlich Schluß mit KDF. Wir können

They are astounding in their numbers and amazing in their feats! The Malmströms are a family of circus performers, and everyone in this huge family has got a story to tell. As they have been in the business for 300 years, there are plenty of riveting tales to be recounted. The family started out as a troupe of tightrope dancers, with one end of their rope tied to the local church's steeple, and the other end fastened to the ground. The founding father of the Malmströms was said to have possessed legendary skills and was able to leap over other performers on his way across the rope!
So as not to lose track of any of their fantastic stories, the family established a museum in their own house in Güstrow, where they have been living since 1917. The visitor is lead by one of the Malmströms through the family circus wagon and through two of the house's rooms, where a story is told to each article that is on display there. There is the story about the famous three Malmströms, the best trapeze artists of their time, and how they once fell, causing Herman to lose his sight. There is the story of the Malmström girls who, after being asked to perform in America, were not allowed to go. Their mother was too worried because, "a rich oil tycoon might have married them, ending there circus career forever!" Then there is the Malmström "bible,"

Zirkuswagen von innen
Interior of the family circus wagon

wieder Artisten sein.“ Dann von den Malmströms, die in Russland auftraten und bei ihrer Heimkehr mit den Russen in Güstrow sprechen konnten. Undundund.
Die Malmströms sind sich sicher, dass ihre Familiengeschichte weit spannender ist als Dallas und Denver zusammen.

a record book of performances written by Grandpa Malmström. At one point it reads in red letters, "Hitler is dead. This means the end of KDF. We can finally be artists again!" (the Nazi KDF was a social program called Kraft Durch Freude, or "Strength Through Enjoyment," which aimed at systemizing the country's leisure and entertainment facilities). There is also the tale of the two Malmströms who, having performed in Russia and having learned the language, were able to speak with the Russian troops who had invaded Güstrow during WWII, helping the town to secure rations. And on and on …
The Malmströms claim that their family history is far more interesting than the 1980's television shows, Dallas and Denver, put together.

Ein Raum voller Geschichten
A room full of stories

Malmström-Museum Güstrow
Zu den Wiesen 17
18273 Güstrow

p: 03843. 680786

e: malmstroem@gmx.de

Kostüm der Tante Emmi, eine beliebte Clownnummer aus den 50er Jahren
Aunt Emmi's costume, part of a popular clown number from the 50's

Zu Hause bei den Wandergesellen

Home of the Wandering Craftsman

Das Herbergsmuseum in Blankenburg im Harz widmet sich einer der schönsten deutschen Traditionen: der Walz. Die ganze Welt ist Lehrmeister für die reisenden Handwerksgesellen. Ein Netzwerk aus Herbergen dient ihnen dabei als Kommunikationshäfen. In ihren weiten Hosen und Hüten treiben sich die Jungs und mittlerweile auch Mädchen nicht nur in Deutschland herum. Schon im 18. Jahrhundert reisten sie so weit sie ihre Neugier trieb und ihre Füße sie trugen. Heute werden sie sogar in Peking gesichtet. Durch bestimmte Rituale gibt sich der Tippelbruder oder die -schwester als solcher oder solche zu erkennen und darf in der Herberge bleiben. Allerdings sind sie an strenge Regeln gebunden. Ohne Arbeit dürfen sie nur sieben Tage an einem Ort bleiben und niemals näher als 50 Kilometer, dem sogenannten Bannkreis, an ihre Heimat herankommen.

Das Herbergsmuseum gibt Einsicht in das Leben auf Wanderschaft, zeigt Reiserouten aus dem vorletzten Jahrhundert, Trachten, Werkzeuge und Ritualgegenstände. Der authentische Fachwerkbau ist die einzige historische Gesellenherberge, die museal erschlossen ist. Und selbst die Wandergesellen kommen hier gerne vorbei.

The Hostel Museum in Blankenburg in the Harz Mountain Region is dedicated to one of Germany's most beautiful traditions, the Walz. It is not the dance that is being referred to here, but the old German tradition of craftsmen taking to the road. The big wide world becomes Meister (teacher or master) to the wandering craftsman. All clad in black flared trousers and big black hats, the traveling handworkers have been going wherever their curiosity and feet have taken them since the 18th Century. In modern times, the young men, and now even women, are not only spotted throughout Germany, but have even been sighted in far away Beijing. A network of hostels serves as a base for communications, and a set of rituals known only to those on the road can open the doors of the special lodges to the craftsmen. Even this life of freedom, however, is subject to strict rules. The wanderers are only allowed to stay in the same place for seven days if without work. They are also required to stay at least 50 km away from their home town at all times.

The museum gives a great deal of insight into life on the road. It shows traveling routes used two centuries ago, as well as clothes, tools and various ritual objects that were used. The authentic old timberwork house in which the exhibit is located is the only historic wanderers' lodge that has been turned into a museum. Even wandering craftsmen like to stop by from time to time, but for no longer than 7 days!

Der Charlottenburger: mulitfunktionales Tuch für die Wanderschaft
The Charlottenburger: multifunctional towel for on the road

Die Kluft der Wandergesellen
The uniform of the wandering craftsmen

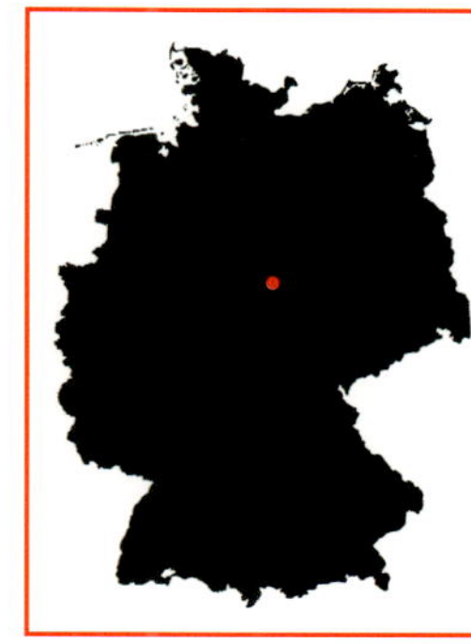

Herbergsmuseum
Hostel Museum
Bergstr. 15
38889 Blankenburg

p: 03944. 365007

f: 03944. 368319

Öffnungszeiten:
Mo bis Do
8.00 – 17.00 Uhr
Fr
8.00 – 13.30 Uhr,
sowie nach Absprache

Opening Hours:
Mon to Thu
8 am – 5pm
Fri
8 am – 1.30 pm,
or by arrangement

Eintritt:
Erwachsene: 1,00 Euro

Entrance Fee:
Adults: 1,00 Euro

Ein altes Herbergszimmer
A room from the old lodge

Viele, viele Nachttöpfe
Lots and lots of chamber pots

Herr Honeckers Schlafgewohnheiten
Mr. Honecker's Sleeping Habits

Im alten Flughangar in Peenemünde, wo einst die Raketenversuche der Nazis durchgeführt wurden, hat sich heute das Pommersche Bettenmuseum angesiedelt. Es mangelt hier weder an Platz noch an Exponaten. Das Museum wirkt wie von einem „Messy" zusammengetragen und dann zu liebevollen Einzelszenarien dekoriert: Stockwerkbetten, Feldbetten, Vier-Mann-Schlafsäcke, Bettpfannen, Ehe-Nachthemden, Aktivitäten im Bett von Sex bis Tod, Flugzeugbetten, Kinderbetten, Gefängnispritschen, Schlafcouche, Strohsäcke, Nachthemden. Es finden sich Antworten auf die Fragen: Wie schläft man im Weltall? Was hat Beate Uhse mit Betten zu tun? Und worauf schlief Honecker im Regierungszug? Wer einen wissenschaftlichen Ansatz erwartet, wird diesen nicht finden. Es werden Anekdoten zur Geschichte des Schlafens geliefert – immerhin, so wirbt das Museum, verbringt der Durchschnittsmensch 33 Prozent seiner Zeit mit dieser Tätigkeit. Der Besucher bewegt sich durch die unzähligen Räume, quetscht sich an Schaufensterfiguren vorbei und entdeckt in jeder Nische etwas Neues. Das Museum ist besucherfreundlich: Die Betten dürfen auch benutzt werden.

The Pomeranian Museum of Beds is in a rather unusual location. The museum is situated in the old aircraft hangar in Peenemünde, where the Nazis used to conduct research trying to develop a new long-range rocket. History aside, the roomy hangar is actually the perfect space for the huge number of exhibits which can be seen here.
The museum works as if arranged by a pack-rat. Organized into separate little scenes, there are bunk beds, camp beds, cots, sleeping bags – for up to four people, bed-pans from by gone ages, cradles, prison pallets, and sofa beds. Among the themes handled here are: how to sleep in outer space, beds and the sex industry, and even how Erich Honecker (socialist party leader in the GDR) slept when travelling on his night train. Those expecting an academic approach will be disappointed. What you will find here are anecdotes related to the history of sleeping. Every human, after all, spends 33% of his or her lifetime sleeping, according to the museum. The visitor moves through numerous rooms, squeezing by mannequins dressed in negligees, discovering something new in every corner. In addition, the museum's curators are very hospitable: guests are free to test out each bed as they please. Sweet dreams.

Bettwärmer: glühende Kohle rein, Bett warm.
Bedwarmers: fill them up with glowing coals, and you have got a warm bed

Viererschlafsack der Armee der DDR
GDR army four-person sleeping bag

Schlafendes Schneewittchen
A sleeping Snow-White

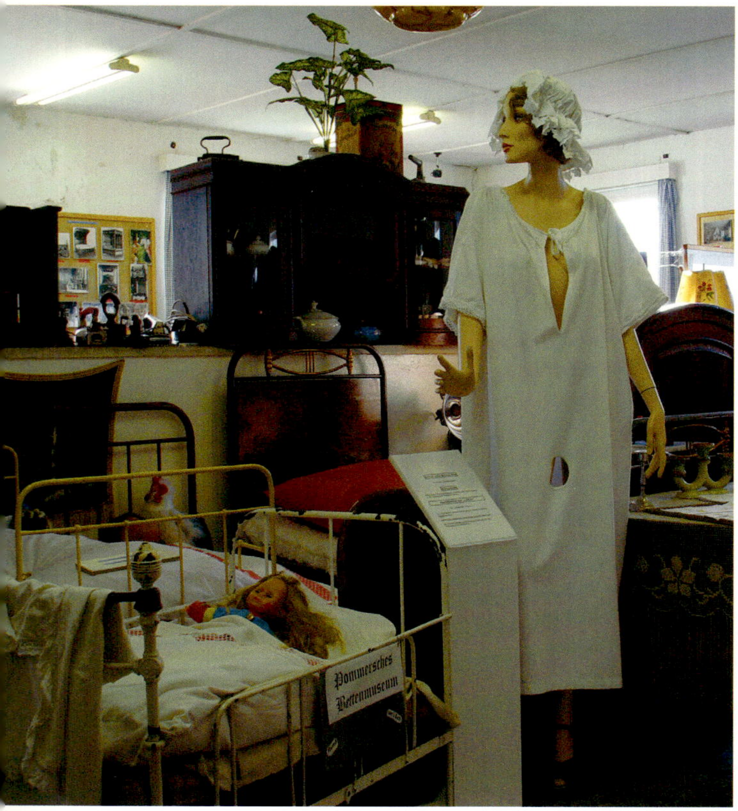

Nachthemd für die Hochzeitsnacht
Wedding night pajamas

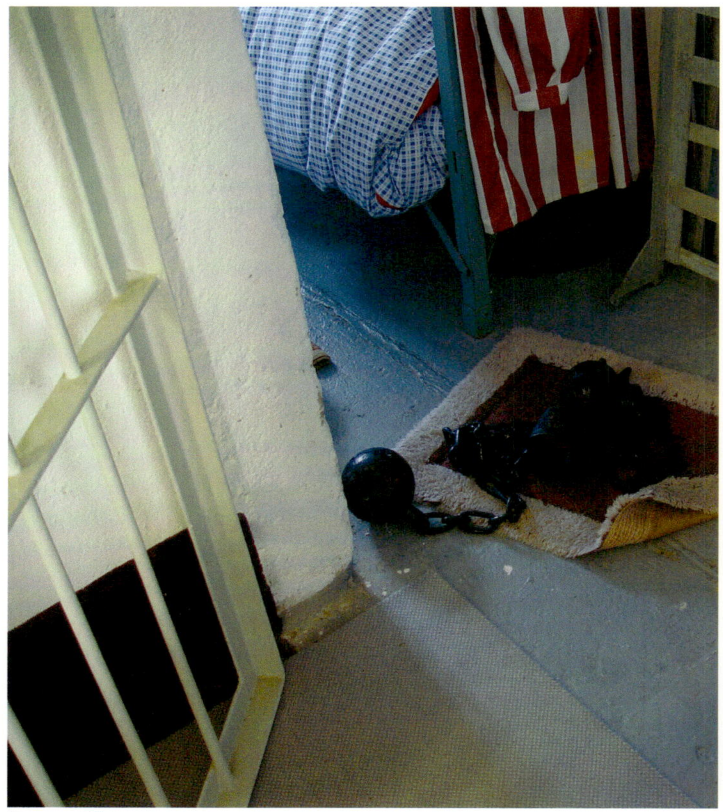

Betten und Ketten
Beds and Chains

Pommersches Bettenmuseum
Pomeranian Museum of Beds
Am Flugplatz
17449 Peenemünde

p: 0171. 9907630
f: 038371. 20352
e: bettenmuseum@peenemuende-info.de

Öffnungszeiten:
April bis Oktober
täglich
10.00 – 18.00 Uhr
Opening Hours:
April to October
daily
10 am – 6 pm

Nach Absprache unter 0171. 9907630 sind Führungen auch außerhalb der Öffnungszeiten möglich.
Guided tours can be arranged outside opening hours: inquiries at 0171. 9907630

Eintritt:
Erwachsene: 3,00 Euro
Kinder: 2,00 Euro
Entrance Fee:
Adults: 3,00 Euro
Children: 2,00 Euro

Erotik pur
Purely erotic

Schirm im Schädel
Umbrella to the skull

Kabinett des Mordes
The Murder Cabinet

Im Institut für Rechtsmedizin der Universität Düsseldorf befindet sich das 1925 gegründete „Criminal Museum". Während im Keller Leichen auf ihre Todesursache hin untersucht werden, wandern die besonders interessanten Stücke ins Museum. Heute sind in der Sammlung über 700 Präparate ausgestellt.

Das Museum ist nicht öffentlich: Es ist nur unter Voranmeldung und mit einem „nachweislichen beruflichen Interesse" zu besichtigen. Einmal im Jahr jedoch, zur „Nacht der Wissenschaft", kann jedermann kommen.

Wir werden in das Museum geführt mit den einfühlsamen Worten, dass dieser Ort sehr wichtig sei, denn „allein 2001 wurden in Nordrhein-Westfalen drei Scheintote wegen mangelnder Fachkenntnis fehlerhaft für tot erklärt und begraben". Die Sammlung dient vor allem der Ausbildung von Ärzten und Polizisten.

Die Ausstellungsstücke sind liebevoll beschriftet, der Besucher kann sich über die unterschiedlichen forensischen Erkenntnisse informieren, wie z.B. über das „Brillen-Hämatom" (ringförmiger Bluterguss um beide Augen: charakteristisch für Schädelbasisbruch), die „stumpfe (im Gegensatz zur scharfen) Gewalt" oder über „Hirnzerreißungen". Interessant sind die Exponaten, die im Zusammenhang mit

Founded in 1925, the "Criminal Museum" is part of the Institute for Forensic Medicine at the University of Düsseldorf. While corpses are analyzed in the basement, the more interesting pieces find their way into the museum, where they are prepared for exhibition. More than 700 pieces are exhibited here.

The museum is not open to the public and can only be visited with advance notification, and with "proven professional interest." It is opened to visitors once a year, however, during the "Night of Science," which usually takes place in November.

We were welcomed to the museum with the following delicate words: "This museum is extremely important. Just last year, three bodies were found in the state of North-Rhine Westphalia. They were wrongly declared dead, and then buried alive." The collection is principally used for training doctors and police officers.

Each piece in the museum is described in gory detail, allowing the interested reader to gain a great deal of insight into forensics and its different techniques. One learns about "Eye-Glass Haematoma," a ring-shaped bruise around both eyes caused by a fracture at the base of the skull, about the difference between a dull hit and a sharp strike, or about

Die Sammlung im Criminal Museum: Jedes Regal birgt neue Schauder
The collection at the Criminal Museum: every cabinet holds another fearful shudder

Erstickungstod stehen: Zu sehen sind die über 200 Schlüssel, die eine Frau geschluckt hat und eine fingergroße Madonna, an der ein Betrunkener erstickt ist. Inspirierend auch die Sammlung ausgefallener Methoden von sexuell bedingten Selbstmorden – Selbststrangulierung rangiert hier ganz oben in der Beliebtheitsskala. Nicht zuletzt sei noch die informative Sektion der Zersetzungsvorgänge an Leichen erwähnt.
Das Museum ist nichts für schwache Nerven. Einen Vorgeschmack kann man auf der Webseite des Institus erhalten.

"brain shredding" – all meticulously explained on information cards. The large section on "death through suffocation" is also quite intriguing. One woman died after eating a set of 200 keys. Another person choked to death, drunken, because he had swallowed a small Madonna icon. The list of causes behind sexual deaths is also inspiring. Self-strangulation seems to have been a hit. Last, but in no way least, is the section on decomposition. The museum is nothing for people with bad nerves. You can get a preview on the institute's web site.

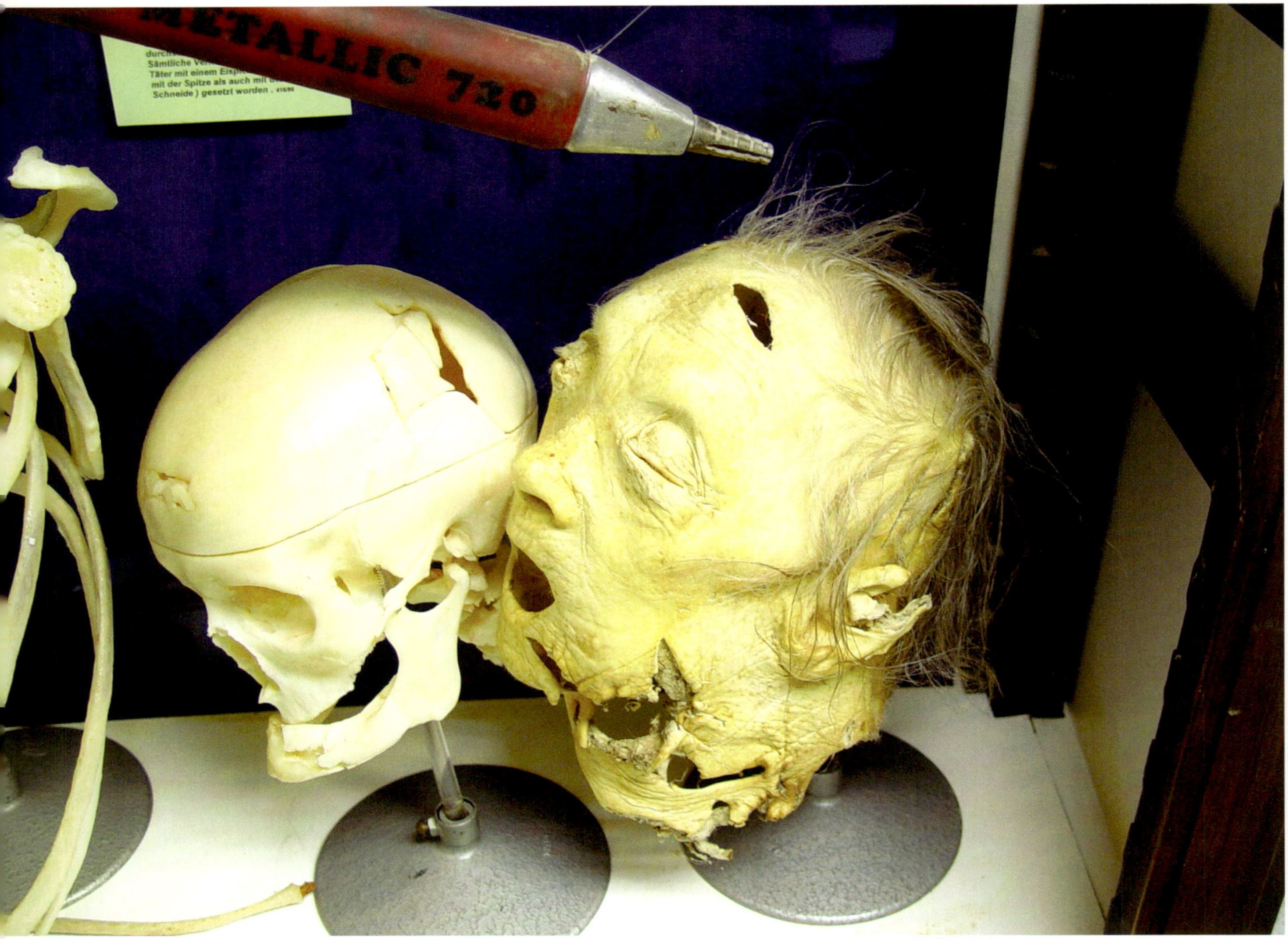

Tödliche Verletzungen durch spitzen Gegenstand
Fatal injuries through pointed objects

Tattoos von Verstorbenen
Tattoos from the deceased

Criminal Museum
Criminal Museum
Moorenstr. 5
40225 Düsseldorf

p: 0211. 8119386

www.uni-duesseldorf. de/
WWW/MedFak/rechtsm/
institut/function/mus/
start.html

Besichtigung nur nach Anmeldung und bei nachweislichem beruflichen Interesse

Visitation only with advanced notification and with proven professional interest

Mit dem Kaiser lernt sich's besser
With the emperor watching, learning is so much easier

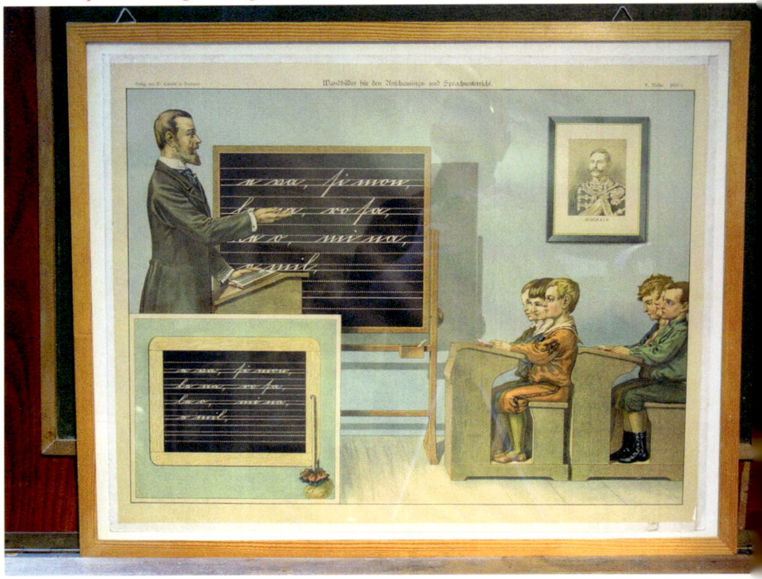

Old School Multimedia
Old School Multimedia

Seit 30 Jahren sammelt das Ehepaar Müller Schaubilder, wie sie im Unterricht verwendet werden. Mittlerweile haben sie über 10 000 davon. Walter Müller, Professor für Pädagogik an der Universität Würzburg, hat sich auf pädagogische Bildmedien spezialisiert. Die Auseinandersetzung mit deren Geschichte gehört zu seinem Arbeitsgebiet und so kann er die Besonderheiten eines jeden Schaubilds erklären. In der Nazi-Zeit beispielsweise wurde selbst bei der Darstellung „harmloser" Märchen Propaganda betrieben: Der Held bei „Dornröschen", der Prinz, ist groß und blond und trägt eine braune Uniform. Vor dem entscheidenden Kuss salutiert er mit dem Hitlergruß. Die böse Fee weist die typischen Juden-Merkmale der damaligen Propaganda auf: krumme Nase, Buckel und schwarze Haare.

Andere Schaubilder klären über medizinische Gefahren auf oder verdeutlichen den Schülern, wie „gutes Benehmen" auszusehen hat. Wieder andere zeigen historische Begebenheiten oder geben ein Bild von fernen Länder und deren Sitten. Herr Müller hat seine ganz eigene Theorie vom Einsatz und Zweck der bildlichen Lehrtafeln, die heute neuen Anschauungsformen weichen müssen. Da ein Poster über mehrere Unterrichtsstunden hinweg im Klassenraum hängt, prägt sich das Bild allmählich in das Gedächtnis der

The Müllers have been collecting school charts for more than 30 years and now have a collection of over 10,000 of these. Walter Müller, who is professor of Education at the nearby University of Würzburg, specializes in educational images. He is especially interested in the historical aspect of the classroom images and can give a fascinating commentary to each of his charts. In the Nazi era for instance, even depictions of "harmless" fairy tales were used to spread propaganda. The hero in Sleeping Beauty was tall and blond, dressed in a brown uniform. Before bending down to kiss the sleeping princess, he took a moment to stop and salute the Führer. The bad fairy in the story was portrayed as being a Jewish person, in fitting with the Nazi stereotype, with a big nose, a hunchback, and black hair.

Other charts explain the medical danger of bad habits or attempt to teach pupils what "good behavior" means. Others illustrate historical scenes or depict strange countries and their customs.

Professor Müller has his own theories about the charts, which seem increasingly to be disappearing in today's classroom. Because a picture is visible throughout the course of numerous consecutive lessons, it becomes slowly and intensely imprinted into the pupil's consciousness – or

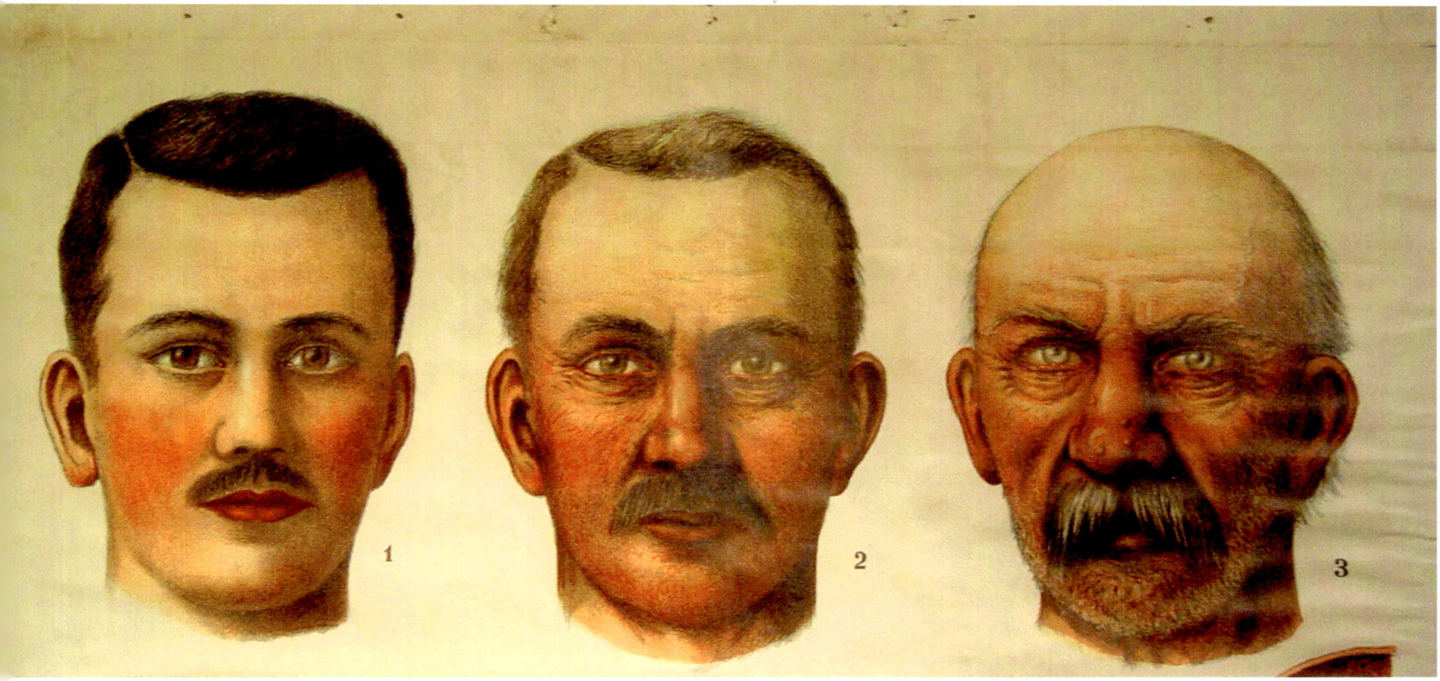

oben: Schaubild, das den Verfall von Alkoholikern erläutert
above: chart showing the decay of an alcoholic

rechts: Schaubild, das auf die Gefahren des Schnürens hinweist
right: chart illustrating the danger of using corsets

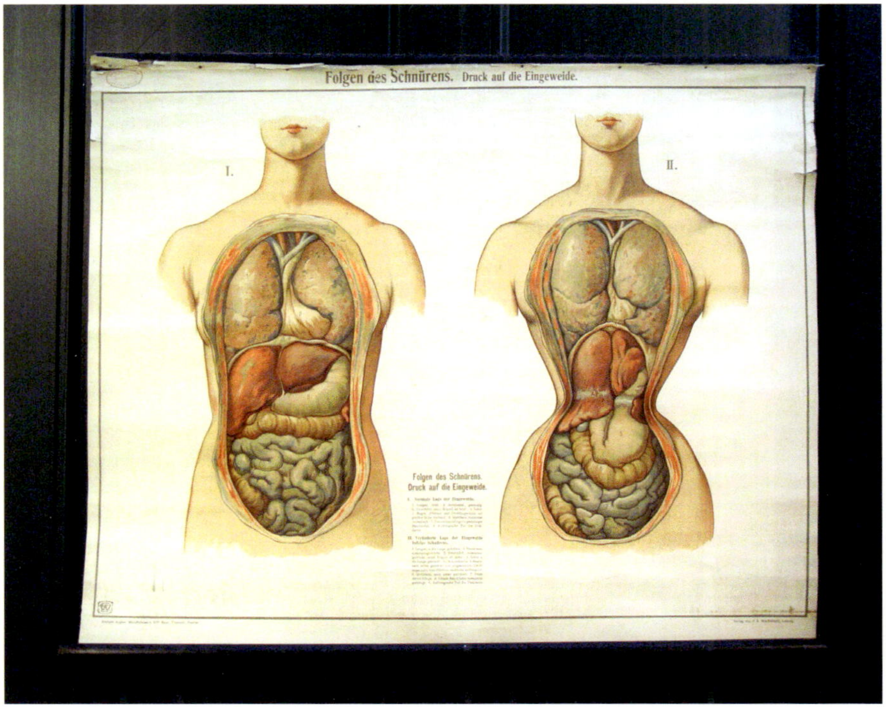

Schüler ein. Das Wissen vertieft sich durch den bildlichen Kontext. Interessant ist, dass diese Bilder häufig in Klassen mit mehreren Altersgruppen verwendet wurden. Sie mussten also anspruchsvoll genug sein, damit es für jeden verständlich war.

Frau Müller dagegen kümmert sich um die Organisation des „Schul-Ladens", einer Mischung aus Museum und Shop: Anhand verschiedener Themengebiete werden antike Lehrmedien gezeigt, und eine alte Schuleinrichtung lädt zum Verweilen ein. Besonders Kinder nutzen dieses Angebot und spielen hier an ihren freien Tagen Schule! Im Laden gibt es Schiefertafeln, Bücher, Kaleidoskope und andere pädagogische Spielereien aus der „Vorzeit" zu kaufen.

sub consciousness – deepening cognitive knowledge of its content. The charts were often used in multiple age group classes and, for this reason, had to illustrate an idea in a way which was both simple and interesting enough for all.

Mrs. Müller runs the "Schul-Laden" ("School Store"), which is a combination of museum and shop. Here you can see old-school teaching material categorized into various topics, or can tarry in a re-created old-time style classroom. The kids in the neighbourhood like to do this, coming over during their holidays to play school. In the store, you can find slates, books, kaleidoscopes, and other "ancient" educational material.

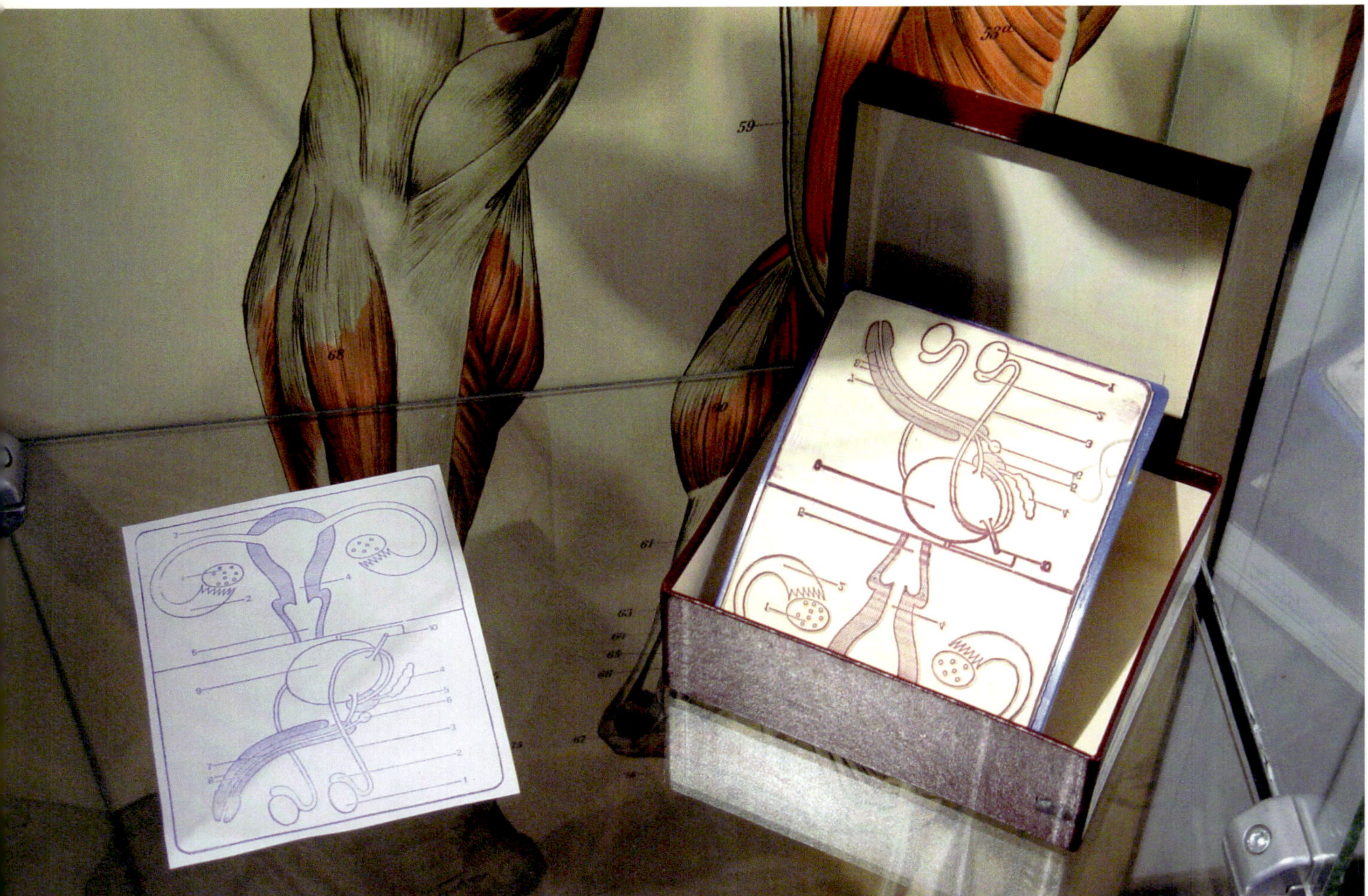

Stempel aus dem Sexualkundeunterricht
A stamp from Sexual Education

Der Schul-Laden
Schule zum Verweilen & Erinnern
The School-Store
A School to stay & to remember

Kolpingstr. 17
97199 Ochsenfurt

p: 09331. 983656

f: 09331. 803918

e: u.m.g.mueller@web.de

www.schul-laden-ochsenfurt.de

Öffnungszeiten:
Di und Mi
10.30 – 13.00 Uhr
Do und Fr
15.00 – 18.00 Uhr
Sa
10.30 – 13.00 Uhr
Während der bayrischen Ferien geschlossen

Opening Hours:
Tue and Wed
10.30 am – 1 pm
Thu and Fri
3 pm – 6 pm
Sat
10.30 am – 1 pm
Closed during Bavarian holidays

Alte Schulbank
An old school bench

bstmedikation:
nn man sich selbst
verordnen.
BIEFFE
MICHELIN

Dr. med.
Konrad Magiera
Apotheken - Notdienst

POLIZEI

Technoland

Techno-Land

Das hängende Dach
The Hanging Roof

Der Architekt Frei Otto hat bei allen seinen Projekten das Prinzip der Minimalflächen angewendet. Er wurde dabei von der Natur inspiriert, in der immer „die allerleichteste Baukonstruktion" vorherrscht.
Auch bei seinen berühmten Zeltdächern ist der Architekt nicht anders vorgegangen. Jeder kennt sein Meisterwerk, die Zeltdächer des Olympiastadions in München. „Geübt" hat der Architekt diese Bauweise am deutschen Pavillon auf der Expo 1967 in Montreal. Er war der Erste, der sich überhaupt mit dem Bau von „hängenden Dächern" beschäftigte. Viele Modelle zeugen von seinen Ideenansätzen. Anfänglich bestanden diese aus Seifenblasen, die durch unterschiedliche Gestelle geformt wurden. Konkretere Modelle entstanden durch Verwendung von Damenstrumpfhosen und Zahnstochern. Die Fachwelt hegte viele Zweifel gegen Ottos Konstruktionsprinzipien. So musste er, als Nachweis seiner Thesen, ein 1:1 Modell seiner Idee bauen. Dieser erste Testaufbau dient heute als Hauptgebäude des „Instituts für leichte Flächentragwerke" in Stuttgart, das Frei Otto 1964 ins Leben rief.
Durch seine natürlichen Formen und Materialien fügt sich das Gebäude in die Landschaft ein. Ein kleiner Bambushain passt gut zur Ästhetik der Anlage. Und wer durchs Fenster schielt, kann das ein oder andere interessante Modell von Frei Otto und seinen Mitarbeitern entdecken. Ruhig klopfen und anfragen, das Dach wird nicht einstürzen.

Inspired by nature, where the "lightest possible construction" dominates, architect Frei Otto applied the principle of minimal planes to all of his projects. This was also the case with his world famous "tent roofs." Almost everybody has seen his masterpiece, the 1972 Olympic Stadium roofs in Munich. The roofs hang from long pillars, looking like big tops.
The architect had "practiced" this kind of roof with the German pavilion for the Expo 1967 in Montreal, and was the first ever to have worked with the principle of hanging roofs. Because in the 1960's, computers were not yet able to calculate such complex constructions, Frei Otto had to work with models. His first models were made of soap bubbles, formed using various frames. More concrete models were then developed using his wife's nylon stockings and toothpicks. In the beginning, many had doubts regarding the safety of Otto's constructions, forcing him to build a full-scale model in order to prove his theories.
This "proof model" is today the home of the "Institute for Lightweight Structures," which was founded by Frei Otto himself in 1964. Through its natural form and material, the building blends perfectly into the surrounding landscape. A small bamboo grove completes the sites aesthetic. If you get a chance to look in through the window, you will be able to see some of the models made by Frei Otto and his team. Do not be afraid to knock and ask if you can have a look. The roof is not going to cave in.

*Institut für Leichtbau
Entwerfen und Konstruieren
Institute for Leightweight
Structures
Pfaffenwaldring 7 und 14
70569 Stuttgart*

p: 0711. 685 6226 -3599

f: 0711. 685 6968 -3789

60 Tonnen Stahl und 700 PS
60 Tons of Steal and 700 H\P

Die Lüneburger Heide ist Deutschlands größtes Naturschutzgebiet. Mitten drin liegt das älteste Manövergelände in Deutschland. Man sollte meinen, dass das ein Widerspruch sei, aber dem ist laut Touristen-Information nicht so: Gerade dort, wo nur Soldaten am Werk sind, gedeihen Fauna und Flora überraschend gut.

Innerhalb dieses militärischen Bereiches befindet sich das Panzermuseum, das zu gleichen Teilen von der Stadt Munster und der Panzertruppenschule der Bundeswehr betrieben wird. Diesen militärischen Einfluss merkt man: Schon in der Eingangshalle wird der Besucher von kernigen Sprüchen begrüßt: „Du fährst einen Panzer, der wenig Gegner hat, aber auch wenig Brüder. Es liegt an Dir, ob ein sprungbereites Raubtier daraus wird oder ein totes Wrack."

Das Museum ist das umfangreichste seiner Art in Europa. Von den Anfängen gepanzerter Fahrzeuge bis hin zu den modernsten Geräten lässt sich hier deutsche Militärgeschichte erfahren – inklusive der Zeit der deutschen Teilung, die sich in unterschiedlichen Panzermodellen wiederspiegelt. Der erste deutsche Panzer, der WOTAN, ist ein „sympathi-

The Lüneburger Heath is Germany's largest nature reserve. Right in the middle of this giant park is also where Germany's oldest military maneuvering field lies. Though this might seem to present a contradiction of sorts, according to the friendly lady at the tourist information center, this is not at all the case.

It is particularly in the areas which can only be accessed by soldiers, where nature is really thriving.Within the confines of this military zone lies the Tank Museum, owned jointly by the army and by the city of Munster.

The military presence is highly visible in the museum. Guests are welcomed with slogans such as this one: "You are driving a tank that has few enemies, but also few brothers. It is up to you, whether you turn it into a ready to jump tiger, or into a lifeless wreck."

The most extensive of its kind in all of Europe, the museum exhibits a huge spectrum of military history, spanning from the earliest tank models to the latest developments in tank technology. Particularly interesting is the period with both East and West German armies, which is reflected in its con-

scher" Klotz aus dem Jahre 1917, der ein wenig so aussieht, als ob lauter Soldaten unter der Metallhülle stehend dieses Ungetüm von Kampfplatz zu Kampfplatz tragen müssten – mit kleinen eleganten Tippelschritten.
Eine militärische Spielzeugsammlung, unzählige Stahlhelme und sogar ein Generalsszepter der Wehrmacht runden die Ausstellung ab. Daneben geben auch die Besucher spannende Anschauungsobjekte ab – es sind meist Veteranen, die sich mit ihren alten Kameraden fachmännisch über die verschiedenen Ausstellungsstücke unterhalten.

trasting models. The first German tank, WOTAN, named after the highest Germanic god, is also on display here. This tank is a cute chunky little piece of metal from 1917.
It gives out the impression that soldiers used to hide underneath it, carrying it from place to place with dainty little soldier steps.
A military toy collection, a huge array of steel helmets, and even the Nazi army General's golden staff can also be viewed here. The visitors are also quite interesting. Most of them are veterans who enjoy discussing the various pieces in the exhibition with their comrades: on a professional level.

Veteranen beim Fachsimpeln
Veterans talking shop

Wotan, der erste Panzer aus dem 1. Weltkrieg
Wotan, the very first tank from WWI

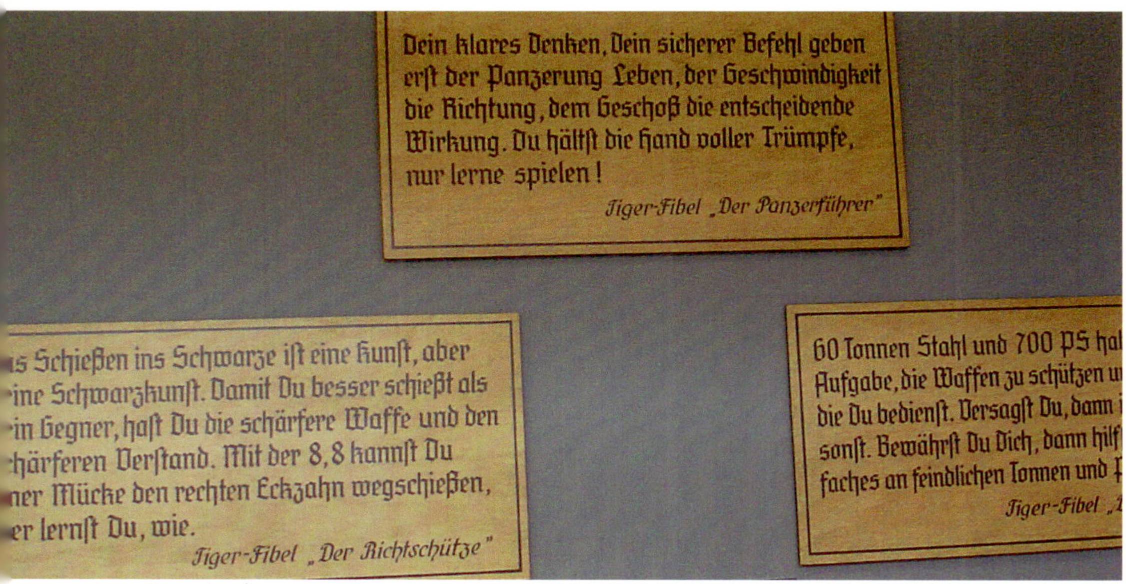

Kernige Sprüche
To the point sayings

Panzermuseum
Tank Museum
Hans-Krüger-Straße 33
29633 Munster

p: 05192. 2552

www.munster.de

Öffnungszeiten:
März bis November:
Di bis So
10.00 – 18.00 Uhr

Opening hours:
March to November:
Tue to Sun
10 am – 8 pm

Eiffelturm im Harz
Eiffel Tower in the Harz

Die Stolberger sind stolz auf ihr Josephskreuz, es ist mit seinen 38 m Höhe das „größte eiserne Doppelkreuz der Welt". Es steht auf einem erloschenem Vulkan, dem Auerberg (579 m). Der Name des Josephskreuz dient nicht als Gedenken an den Heiligen Joseph, sondern erinnert an den Grafen Joseph von Stolberg, der den Turm errichten ließ.
Dank des herrlichen Panoramablicks von der Spitze des Auerbergs auf die Harzregion, stand hier schon im 17. Jahrhundert ein Aussichtsturm. Doch wurde der Turm bald Opfer des Wetters: Eine Sage berichtet von Stürmen, die wie auf „einer wilden Jagd um den Turm rasten".
So musste der erste Turm wegen Schäden durch viele „wilde Jagden" 1768 abgerissen werden. Knapp 60 Jahre später beauftragte der Graf von Stolberg den Berliner Stararchitekten Karl Friedrich Schinkel, einen neuen Turm zu entwerfen. Schinkel setze ein hölzernes Doppelkreuz auf den Berg, das nur durch Leitern zu erklettern war. Die Investition in das Kreuz lohnte sich – der Tourismus blühte auf und keine vier Jahre später konnte der erste Gasthof auf dem Auerberg eröffnen. Doch 1880 wurde auch dieses Kreuz bei einem starken Unwetter umgerissen.
Sechs Jahre später hatten der Graf und der Harzklub genug Gelder für einen Wiederaufbau gesammelt: Das neue Kreuz sollte das von Schinkel übertreffen! Die Weltausstellung in Paris war gerade beendet und der Eiffelturm als grazile Technologie-Errungenschaft gerühmt. So etwas sollte auch auf dem Auerberg stehen! Im August 1886 stand der neue Turm. Er ähnelte dem hölzernen Doppelkreuz Schinkels, war aber mit 100 000 Nieten und 128 Tonnen Eisen doch ein anderes Kaliber – und die Touristen bewiesen dies.
Zu Zeiten der DDR wurde das Kreuz nie restauriert und 1987 behördlich gesperrt. Ein Jahr nach der Wende wurde der Turm renoviert, was zeigt, wie wichtig das größte eiserne Doppelkreuz der Welt für die Region ist.

The people of Stolberg are quite fond of their Joseph's Cross Tower. Mounted on the top of an extinct volcano, the Auerberg (579 m – the neighborhood mountain of Stolberg), with its 38 m height, it is said to be the "world's biggest iron double cross." The lookout tower was named not after a holy man, but in remembrance of its patron, Joseph von Stolberg.
On top of the Auerberg, you can enjoy a magnificent view over the mountainous Harz region. The mountain's first watchtower was built there back in the 17th century. Exposed to harsh weather conditions however, it had to be torn down in 1768. A local legend reports of storms which were "like a wild hunt, furiously attacking the tower."
In 1832, Lord Joseph commissioned the famous architect, Karl Friedrich Schinkel, to design a new tower. Schinkel placed a wooden double cross on top of the mountain, and the new tower could only be scaled using a wooden ladder. The investment turned out to be profitable. Tourism boomed in response to the tower, and four years after its construction, an inn was even opened nearby. Unfortunately, the storms did not decrease. The tower was destroyed in one of these in 1880.
Six years later, von Stolberg and the "Harz Club" had collected enough money to rebuild again, this time deciding to insure stability and safety against the terrible weather. Inspired by the construction that same year of the Eiffel Tower in Paris, and using the same technology, architect Otto Beißwänger designed a tower, which, though looking similar to Schinkel's tower, was slightly bigger, being built with over 100,000 rivets and 128 tons of steal.
Sadly, the cross was not taken care of during the time of the GDR, and it had to be closed in 1987 due to structural damage. Just one year after the fall of the Berlin wall however, the tower was fully renovated, showing how important the world's biggest iron double cross is, at least for the region of Stolberg.

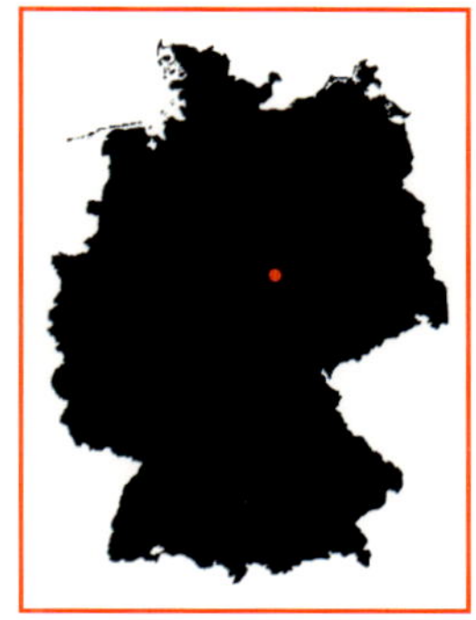

Das weltgrößte eiserne Doppelkreuz in Stolberg
The world's biggest double iron cross in Stolberg

Josephskreuz
zwischen / between
06547 Stolberg/Harz
und / and
06507 Güntersberge

Vom Parkplatz ca. 20 minütige Wanderung

20 minutes stroll away from the parking lot

Öffnungszeiten:
Täglich
9.00 – 16.30 Uhr

Opening hours:
Daily
9 am – 4.30 pm

Touristeninformation
Markt 2
06547 Stolberg / Harz

p: 034654. 454

Es werde Licht!

Let there be Light!

Jeden Abend um 23 Uhr, nachdem der Nachtwächter sein Lied gesungen und seine Runde gedreht hat, gehen in Dinkelsbühl alle öffentlichen Lichter aus. Wer dann noch mittelalterliche Gebäude, Stadtmauer, Stadtgraben und Stadtpark im Flutlicht erleben will, wird dies in Dinkelsbühl dennoch tun können – mit dem Stadtbeleuchtungsautomat. Dieser ist ein kleines Kästchen, das auf einer Seitenwand der Schranne, des alten Festsaals von Dinkelsbühl, angebracht ist. Wie bei allem in Dinkelsbühl weist ein in Fraktur verfasster Schriftzug (selbst die Döner-Imbissläden haben hier altdeutsche Schriftzüge, wie Istanbul-Grill) auf das unscheinbare Kästchen hin: Stadtbeleuchtung. Man klappt es auf, wirft 4 Euro (bitte zwei 2-Euromünzen bereithalten, das Kästchen reagiert sonst nicht) hinein, dreht an einer Schraube, wartet ca. 1 Minute lang und tatsächlich – trara – alle Flutlichter der Stadt schalten sich ein, und noch einmal ist die Stadt in ihrer ganzen Pracht zu sehen. Für zwei Stunden: also genug Zeit, um alle Sehenswürdigkeiten abzugrasen oder sich auf ein Stelldichein in den Park vor die Stadtmauer zu begeben und dort der oder dem Liebsten ins Ohr zu flüstern: Die Stadt leuchtet nur für dich.
Immerhin liegt Dinkelsbühl auf der Romantischen Straße und das ist Dinkelbühls Anwort darauf…
Die meisten Touristen bleiben übrigens schon in Rothenburg o. d. Tauber hängen, so dass Dinkelsbühl tatsächlich Romantik bewahrt hat. Im Gegensatz zu Rothenburg wird hier der Einzelhandel von Bürgern betrieben und nicht von angereisten Souvenirhändlern. So wirkt Dinkelsbühl nicht nur echt, sondern ist es auch.

Every night at 11 o'clock p.m., after the night watchman has sung his song and made his last rounds, all the public lights go out. That does not mean, however, that it is no longer possible to see the beautiful mediaeval town of Dinkelsbühl, with its old buildings, city wall, moat, and park, fully illuminated. This can still be achieved – with the help of the city light vending machine.
This apparatus is a small metal box, mounted on the outer wall of the Schranne, or town hall. Gothic lettering, which adorns all of Dinkelsbühl's signs (including the Turkish kebab stand's Istanbul Grill sign) points out the box. Throw in 4 Euros (make sure to keep two 2 Euro coins handy, otherwise the miracle will not happen), twist the handle, wait for about one minute, and ta da! The floodlights switch slowly on.
The town can now be seen in all its nocturnal glory for another two hours! This allows for enough time to check out all of the sightseeing spots, or to go for a romantic walk through the park. Just whisper tenderly into your beloved's ear, telling them that the light shines for them, and for them alone. Dinkelsbühl is found after all on the "Romantische Straße," the romantic road that weaves through this part of the country…
Most tourists seem to get stuck in the nearby town of Rothenburg o. d. Tauber, also to be found on the romantic road. This is much to the annoyance of Dinkelsbühl's Manager of Tourism, but, on the other hand, allows the romance to stay in town. The local stores are still local stores. There are no souvenir shops run by ex-Japanese tourists. In this way, Dinkelsbühl does not only feel real, it is real.

Der Nachtwächter: nachdem er seine Runde gedreht hat, wirds dunkel
The Night Watchman: after he finishes making his rounds, the lights go out

Das Kästchen mit dem Automaten für die Stadtbeleuchtung
The box holding the automat for the city's lights

Stadtbeleuchtung Dinkelsbühl
Dinkelsbühl Citylights
Automat an der Schranne
Am Marktplatz
91550 Dinkelsbühl

Der Automat ist an der Längsseite der Schranne, auf der der Touristeninformation weggekehrten Seite.

The automat is to be found on the side wall of the Schranne, not the one facing the tourist office.

Dinkelsbühl im Glanze der Stadtbeleuchtung
Dinkelsbühl in the full brilliance of its city lights

Ebstorf und wie es die Welt sah

The World According to Ebstorf

Im Kloster zu Ebstorf fand man 1830 beim Aufräumen eine Weltkarte, deren Entstehung auf das 13. Jahrhundert datiert wird. Mit ihren 12,75 Quadratmetern ist sie heute die größte und reich illustrierteste Weltkarte des Mittelalters. Nach dem sensationellen Fund wurde die Karte nach Hannover zur Untersuchung geschickt und dort während des Zweiten Weltkrieges bei einem Bombenangriff zerstört. Anhand von Fotografien und Skizzen konnte eine originalgetreue Nachbildung angefertigt werden. Diese hängt jetzt wieder im Kloster und ist der Stolz der mittlerweile evangelischen Konventualinnen, die sie interessierten Besuchern gerne erklären. Die Welt wird symbolisch durch die Gestalt von Jesus zusammengehalten. Entsprechend mittelalterlichen Darstellungen als Scheibe, die oben den Osten, unten den Westen und im Zentrum die Stadt Jerusalem aufweist. Die Karte zeigt als Sinnbild der Weltauffassung der damaligen Zeit den erdkundlichen, geografischen und naturkundlichen Wissensstoff zusammen mit dem biblischen und antiken mythologischen Gedankengut in einem Bild. Bedeutende Städte wie Rom finden sich daher ebenso, wie die Arche Noah auf dem Berg Ararat. Die Stadt Kolchis hat das goldene Vlies ans Stadttor genagelt. Auch das Paradies ist verzeichnet und gleich daneben eine Sammlung von seltsamen Menschen, die man damals in Afrika vermutete: z. B. Menschen mit Armen, die aus den Ohren wachsen. Etwas verwunderlich erscheint, dass neben den klassischen Städten auch das Kloster Ebstorf (Ebbekestorpe) und umliegende Gemeinden dargestellt sind. So könnte die Karte wohl als Lern- und Lehrbild für die Nonnen gedient haben. Auch ihr Kloster gehört zur Welt des Herrn. Wahrscheinlich wurde die Karte von den Nonnen im Kloster angefertigt – auf 30 Blättern Pergamentpapier gemalt und dann zusammengenäht.

Die Karte, so wird vermutet, geht auf Gervarius von Tilbury, der möglicherweise identisch mit dem damaligen Ebstorfer Probst Gervasius sein könnte, zurück. Er war ein Berater von Otto IV. und ein weit gereister Mann.

In the late Benedictine Cloister at Ebstorf in the year 1830, somebody found a map of the world while cleaning. The map is almost 13 square meters large and dates back to the 14th century. It is the biggest and most richly illustrated map of the middle ages.

This sensational find was sent off to Hannover for analysis, where it was later destroyed in a bombing raid during the Second World War. Luckily, with help from photographs that had been taken, and sketches that had been made, the map could be re-drawn into a faithful reproduction. This is now hanging in the cloister at Ebstorf, where, instead of being hidden away, it is the great pride of the now protestant nuns who live there. They are more than happy to explain all that they know about the map.

The earth is represented by a round disc, which is being held by Jesus. To the top is the East, to the bottom is the West, and in the center of the map is Jerusalem. The map is revealing of the impressive knowledge and beliefs of the people of that era. Cities like Rome are to be expected. More unusual though, is that Noah's Ark can be found on the map, on top of the mountain Ararat. The city Kolchis has a city gate decorated with Golden Fleece. Paradise is also shown on the map, and right next to that, there is a group of strange looking creatures, who were believed to have lived in Africa: people with arms growing out of their ears. The cloister itself and its surrounding areas are also included, standing among the great cities of the world. The map must have served as a great instructional tool for the nuns – their cloister belonged to God's world too.

Probably drawn up by the nuns themselves, the map was painted onto 30 different sheets of parchment, and then sewn together. It is believed to have been designed by Gervarius von Tilbury, the bishop at the time. He was advisor to Otto IV, and a well traveled man.

Kloster Ebstorf
Dominican Cloister
Kirchplatz 10
29574 Ebstorf

p: 05822. 2304

Die Ebstorfer Weltkarte
The Ebstorf World Map

Hier spielten noch bis 1989 Kinder aus der Sowjetunion
Children from the Soviet Union played here up until 1989

Back in the USSR

Back in the USSR

Südöstlich von Berlin, wo sich das Graffiti auf Hakenkreuze reduziert und Skinheads aus fahrenden Autos herausgrölen, liegt Wünsdorf. Heute ähnelt der Ort einer Geisterstadt, bis zur Wende aber lebten hier zeitweise 100 000 sowjetische Soldaten. Wünsdorf, oder Wjunsdorf, war die Zentrale der Westgruppe der sowjetischen Armee. Ein Zug verkehrte täglich nach Moskau. Das Leben hier war sowjetisch geprägt: die sowjetische Zivilbevölkerung hinterließ 450 streunende Katzen. Zwischen den Bäumen sieht man noch hier und da Kosmonautenstatuen in Heldenpose. Ein Staat im Staat. DDR-Bürgern war der Zutritt strengstens untersagt und die nahe gelegene Bundesstraße machte einen großen Bogen um die Kasernenstadt.

Die Geschichte des Militärs zieht sich wie ein roter Faden durch die Geschichte von Wünsdorf. Neben den Ruinen der Sowjet-Baracken stehen hier noch 19 Spitzbunker aus dem Zweiten Weltkrieg, sie erinnern in ihrer Form an Stupas aus dem Himalaya, waren aber als Schutz für das Oberkommando des deutschen Heers gebaut, das hier seinen Hauptsitz hatte. Maybach und Zeppelin sind unwiderruflich mit Wünsdorf verknüpft. Unterirdische Bunkeranlagen, Schießplätze, all das prägt das Bild Wünsdorfs. Und dann gibt es da noch einen versteckten Friedhof mit

South-east from Berlin, where the graffiti has been reduced down to swastikas, and where skinheads hang out of car windows as they drive by, lies the city of Wünsdorf. These days, the city seems to be a ghost town, but before the wall fell, 100,000 Russians lived here. Wünsdorf, or Wjunsdorf, was the headquarters of the Soviet army's West Group.

A train traveled daily from Wünsdorf to Moscow, and life here was greatly influenced by Soviet culture. The Soviet civil population left 450 stray cats behind them, as well as a number of cosmonaut statues standing among the trees in heroic poses. A state within a state, access to the city was strictly barred to citizens of the GDR. The nearby state highway made a huge curve, going out of its way to bypass the barrack town.

Military history is deeply entwined with the story of Wünsdorf, running like a red thread through the city's past. Near the ruins of the Soviet barracks, there are still 19 high quality pointed bunkers from the Second World War. They remind one in their form of the Himalayan stupa, but were actually built as protection for the elite Oberkommando, or High Command, who continued to give out their orders in safety. Maybach and Zeppelin have also left their irreversible imprint on the city, underground bunker complexes

Ein sowjetischer Kosmonaut
A Soviet Cosmonaut

Grabplatten in seltsamen Schriften: Zwischen 1914 und 1921 wurden hier Kriegsgefangene, darunter etliche Sikhs, Hindus und Muslime, interniert und auf dem örtlichen Friedhof begraben.
Nach der Wende versuchte man, Wünsdorf positiv zu belegen. Es nennt sich heute Bücherstadt und nicht mehr Kasernenstadt. In den Baracken befinden sich Antiquariate. Der militärische Schatten aber bleibt hängen.

being named after them. Shooting grounds complete the picture. Not to forget, there is also a hidden cemetery with gravestones in Arabic writing. Between 1914 and 1921, prisoners of war were held here, among others, various Sikhs, Hindus and Muslims. Wünsdorf was a stationing base for troops even back during the time of the Emperor.
After the Berlin wall came down, the attempt was made to bring something more positive to Wünsdorf. Today, the town is trying to make a name for itself as Book Town instead of Barrack Town. In the old barracks, various shops for antique books have been enlisted. The military shadow, however, still seems to somehow hang over Wünsdorf.

Ein Spitzbunker: Bomben prallen an ihm ab
A pointed bunker: Bombs just ricochet right off of it

Lenin vor dem ehemaligen Offizierskasino
Lenin in front of the former officers casino

15838 Wünsdorf

www.garnisonsmuseum-wuensdorf.de

Altes Bahngleis: Von hier gab es bis 1989 täglich eine Direktverbindung nach Moskau
Old train tracks: these tracks were part of a direct connection to Moscow until 1989

Berühmte Tiere

Famous Animals

Der Mecklenburger Pfeilstorch

The Arrow-Stork from Mecklenburg

Am 21. Mai 1822 konnte dank eines ungewöhnlichen Fundes bei Klütz in Mecklenburg endlich ein großes zoologisches Rätsel gelöst werden: Was tut der Storch im Winter? Lange Zeit spekulierte die Wissenschaft über den Verbleib dieser Vögel: Hielten sie Winterschlaf, versteckten sie sich, oder flogen sie gar nach Afrika? Bewiesen werden konnte nichts, und der Diskussionen gab es viele.

Das änderte sich schlagartig, als in Mecklenburg ein „Pfeilstorch" gefunden wurde: Im Hals des sonst noch recht munteren Storchs steckte ein afrikanischer Pfeil! Dieser Vogel galt fortan als Beweis dafür, dass der Storch sich im Winter nach Afrika zurückzieht. Der reichverzierte afrikanische Pfeil hatte sich nur durch die Haut des Storchenhalses gebohrt und dabei keine lebenswichtigen Organe verletzt.

Auf ihren 10- bis 14-tägigen Reisen brauchen die Störche keine Nahrung zu sich zu nehmen, sie müssen noch nicht einmal schlafen. So konnte der Storch mit seinem Pfeil im Hals ohne Probleme bis nach Mecklenburg gelangen.

Hier angekommen, war der Pfeil recht hinderlich bei der Jagd auf Frösche, und so musste der arme Storch jämmerlich verhungern. Mittlerweile wurden an die 20 Pfeilstörche in Deutschland entdeckt, aber keiner wurde so liebevoll ausgestopft und der Öffentlichkeit präsentiert wie der „Meck-

On May 21st, 1822, due to a discovery in Klütz, in the north of Germany, one of the greatest mysteries in modern zoology was able to be solved – the question: What do storks do in the winter? Scientists had been speculating for ages about the whereabouts of storks in wintertime. Do they hibernate? Are they just hiding? Or do they even fly all the way to Africa? Experts disputed endlessly, but no theory could be proved. This all changed when, in the Mecklenburg region (Northern Germany), an "arrow-stork" was found, an otherwise happy, healthy bird, with an African arrow sticking out of the side of its neck. The beautifully decorated arrow had only pierced the bird's skin, not damaging any vital organs. This, in combination with the fact that storks do not need any food or sleep on their 10 to 14 days journey from Africa to Europe, allowed the arrow pierced bird to survive the trip. Once the determined stork made it to Mecklenburg, however, because the arrow was no small hindrance in the fowl's hunt for frogs, the poor bird starved to death.

Up until now, about 20 of these arrow-storks have been recovered, but only the one from Mecklenburg has been so neatly taxidermied and presented to the public. The "Mecklenburger Pfeilstorch" (Mecklenburg Arrow-Stork)

Storch mit afrikanischem Pfeil im Hals
Stork with African arrow in neck

lenburger Pfeilstorch", den man heute in der Zoologischen Sammlung der Universität Rostock bewundern kann. Die ist nicht nur des Storches wegen sehenswert. In den letzten hundert Jahren wurde das Ausstellungsdesign nicht erneuert. In unzähligen Vitrinen findet man eine der größten zoologischen Sammlungen der Welt, mit einigen wirklich seltenen Exemplaren. Daneben gibt es eine ständige Ausstellung zum Thema „Kulturzoologie", in der Handschuhe aus gewebter Muschelseide und ein „echtes Einhorn" (der Stoßzahn eines Narwals) zu sehen sind.

can be seen in the zoological collection at the University of Rostock. Not only interesting because of the stork, the place holds one of the largest taxidermy collections in the world. Some of its pieces are even internationally renowned. There is a permanent exhibit about "Cultural Zoology," which shows gloves made of shell silk, as well as a "real unicorn's horn," reminding us why poachers get as much as they do for narwhale tusks.

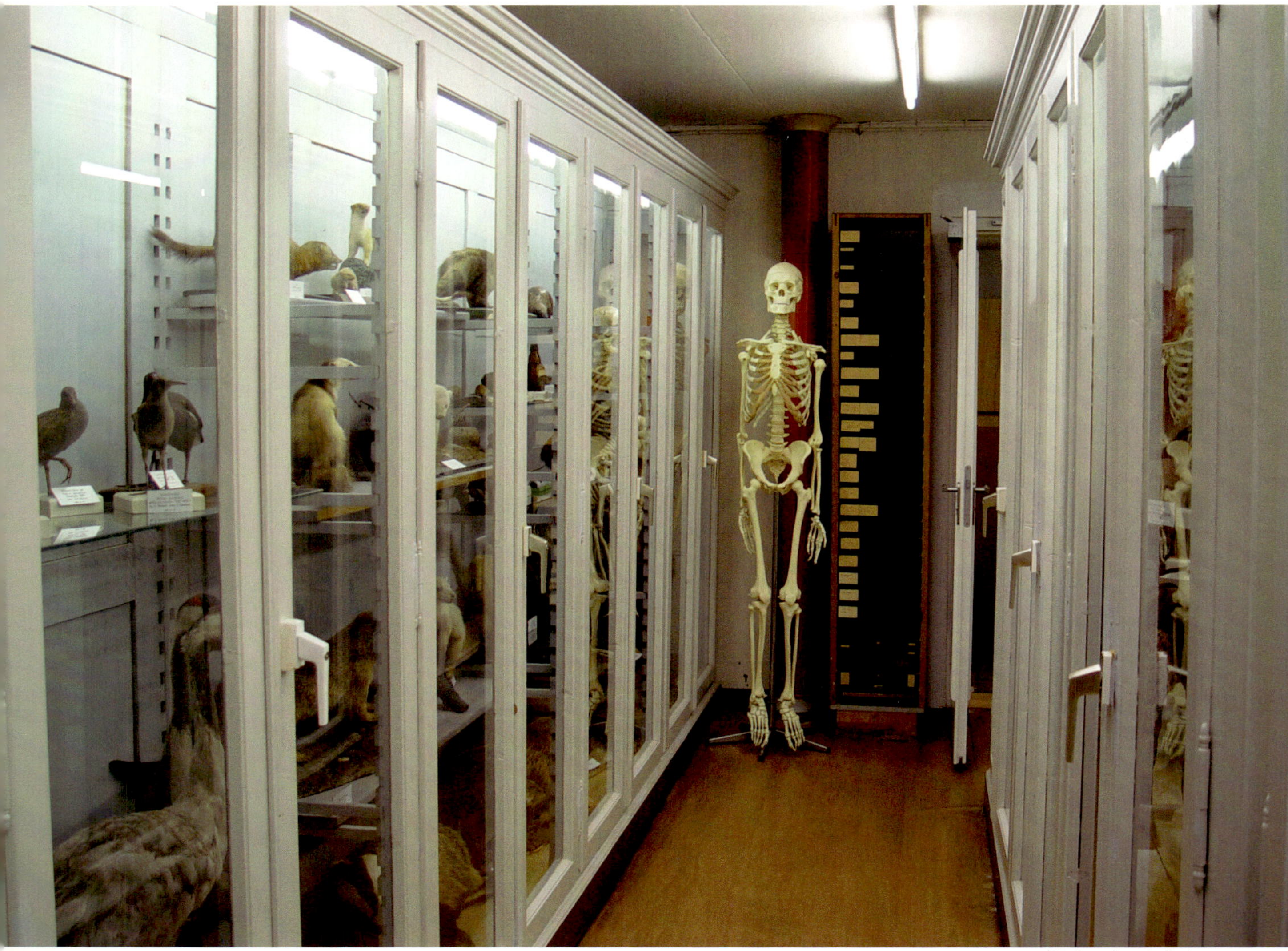

Die Sammlung des Instituts
The institute's collection

Ein Kinderskelett
A child's skeleton

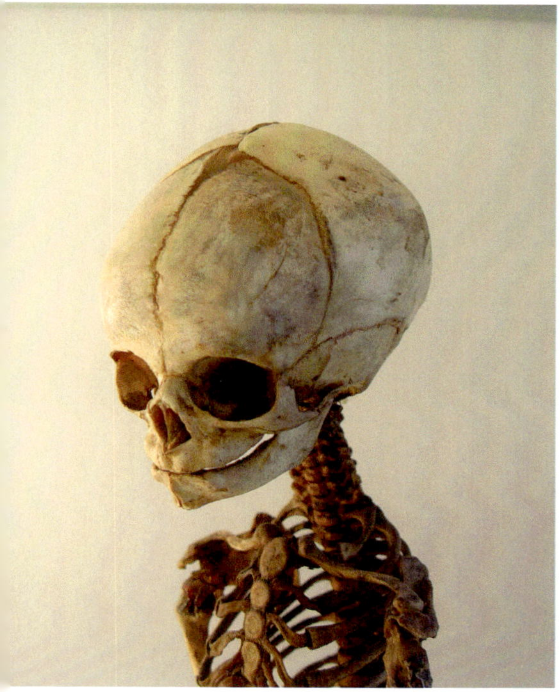

Handschuhe aus Muschelseide
Gloves made of oyster silk

Universität Rostock, Fachbereich Biowissenschaften, Institut für Biodiversitätsforschung, Allgemeine und Spezielle Zoologie
University of Rostock, Faculty of Life Science Institute of Biodiversity Research, Department of Zoology
Universitätsplatz 2
18055 Rostock

p: 0381. 4986281

f: 0381. 4986262

www.biologie.uni-rostock.de/zoologie/main.html

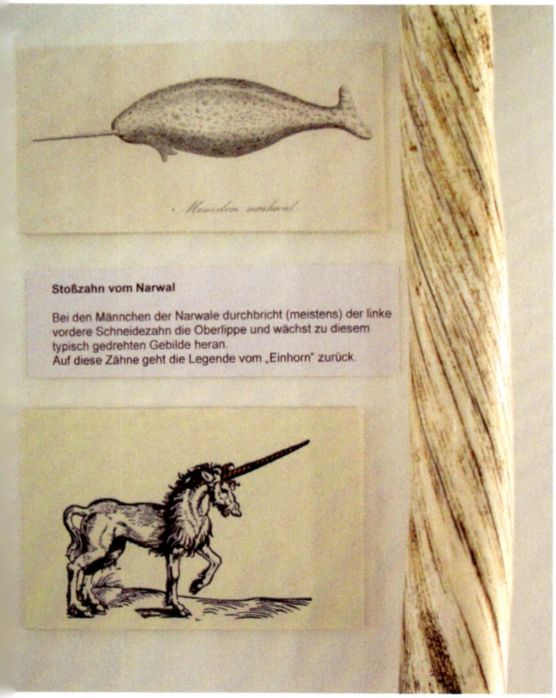

Das Horn eines Narwales
The horn of a Narwhale

Ausgestopfte Affen
Stuffed apes

Der Mops ohne Schwanz
The Mutt with No Tail

Der berühmteste Mensch der verschlafenen Fachwerkstatt Bretten im Kraichgau war ein gewisser Philipp Schwarzerdt, auf altgriechisch ‚Melanchthon' genannt und als solcher auch bekannt. Er war einer der führenden Humanisten und Mitstreiter Luthers. Ihm zu Ehren wird Bretten auch gerne die „Melanchthonstadt" genannt.
Brettens zweitbekannteste historische Figur war ein Zeitgenosse Melanchthons, und auch er ist nicht unter seinem wirklichen Namen, sondern nur als „das Hundle" bekannt – man befindet sich im Badischen. Um ihn nicht zu vergessen, errichtete man in Bretten einen Brunnen in der Melanchthonstraße.
Das Hundle ist dick und klein und schaut etwas dusselig von seinem hohen Pfeiler auf den Brunnen herunter. Außerdem fehlt ihm der Schwanz. Den hat es an den Herzog Ulrich von Württemberg bei der Belagerung Brettens 1504 verloren.
Der Sage nach wurden die Brettener von Ulrich von Württemberg belagert. Der Bürgermeister hatte den grandiosen Einfall, einen Hund zu mästen und ihn dann, dick und fett, vor die Stadttore zu schicken: Die Belagerer sollten denken, dass man noch allerhand Futter in der Stadt hätte. Gesagt getan, und nach ein paar Wochen war aus dem Hund ein praller Fettwanst geworden.
Und tatsächlich, der Trick funktionierte: Etwas verärgert hieben die Belagerer dem Hundle den Schwanz ab, und brachen alsbald ihre Zelte ab. Den Brettenern ging's fortan gut. Und das Hundle findet man heute als Abschluss auf einem der Strebepfeiler an der Südseite der Pfarrkirche, ebenso wie auf dem besagten Brunnen.
In den 60er Jahren gab es noch viele Souvenirs und Wappen, die das Hundle schmücken durfte, heute scheint das Wahrzeichen aus der Mode gekommen zu sein.

The most famous person to come out of the small and cozy town of Bretten, close to the Black Forest, was a man named Philipp Schwarzerdt, better known by his Greek name, Philipp Melanchthon. Melanchthon was a great humanist and reformer as well as a close friend and confident of Martin Luther. In honour of this great citizen, Bretten is also sometimes called Melanchthonstadt, or Melanchthon City.
The second most famous character to come out of Bretten was not a person at all, but a dog. Like Melanchthon, he was also given a pseudonym, his real name being forgotten. The heroic figure is known as "das Hundle," or "little dog," and was forever memorialized by a fountain in the Melanchthonstraße (Melanchthon Street), in Bretten.
Perched on top of a pillar, a likeness of the fat little dog sits looking down at the fountain with a strange expression on its face. Stranger still is that the dog's tail is missing. This is because it was lost in an encounter with Duke Ulrich von Württemberg during the siege of Bretten in 1504.
According to legend, the citizens of Bretten were on the brink of starvation and suffering heavily under the siege. The town's Mayor then had a brilliant idea. He decided to use the town's last rations to fatten up a dog. Once nicely fattened, the plump little dog was to be sent outside of the town's gate. The besiegers were then supposed to surmise that the town was continuing to hold out and doing well, having so much food that they could even feed the dogs. After a couple weeks of gorging, the chubby hero was sent out on his mission. Amazingly enough, the plan actually worked. Disheartened and annoyed, the town's besiegers cut off the dog's tail, and then disappeared, leaving the people of Bretten in peace. From this day on, the people of Bretten lived happily ever after and built a fountain in gratitude to the mutt who had saved them. This gratitude continued on all the way up until the 1960's, when souvenirs and emblems commemorating the Hundle could be found throughout the town. Sadly, the little fellow seems to have gone out of fashion these days.

Das treue Möpsle
The faithful mutt

Stadtinformation Bretten
City Information Bretten
Am Marktplatz 12
75015 Bretten

p: 07252. 957620

www.bretten.de

Hundle's Brunnen
The Dog's Fountain
Am alten Markt 12
75015 Bretten

Hundle's Statue
The Dog's Statue
Johannes Kirche
(außen / outside)
Kirchgasse 12
75016 Bretten

Der Brunnen mit Möpsle
The fountain with the mutt

Der innere Schweinehund

The Inner Pig

Wem beim „Vertreiben des inneren Schweinehundes“ die Vorstellungskraft fehlt, sich dieses ungeheuerliche Tierchen bildlich vorzustellen, fahre am Besten nach Altenkirchen auf Rügen und gehe dort in die alte Kirche: auf der Wand ist er aufgemalt. Die ihn schon öfter verjagt haben, werden ihn sofort als solchen wieder erkennen.

Am etwa 1200 errichteten Backsteinbau der Kirche (übrigens einer der ältesten im gesamten Ostseeraum) lässt sich noch so manche Geschichte aus längst vergangenen Tagen ablesen. In einem Vorraum der Kirche ist der Svantevit-Stein, ein Stein mit einer Männerfigur mit Horn eingemauert. Rügenkenner wissen, dass auf dem Kap Arkona zwischen 1068 und 1168 das größte westslawische Heiligtum stand, die Jaromisburg mit Tempelanlage für den vierköpfigen Gott Svantevit. Über 300 Tempeldiener bewachten hier die Tempelschätze. Die Slawen fühlten sich sicher vor Eroberungen vom Land und hatten nicht mit den Dänen gerechnet, die 1163 vom Meer her angriffen. Die Tempelanlage fiel und die christliche Religion wurde eingeführt. Für das Volk bedeutete dies konkret, dass sie ihren Zehnten nun nicht mehr an den Oberpriester, sondern an den Bischof abgeben mussten. Die Kirche von Altenkirchen musste, um diesen Paradigmenwechsel aufzuzeigen, mit vielen Symbolen bestückt werden. So auch mit dem inneren Schweinehund. Er rennt dem Ausgang zu und lässt die Tatkraft der ersten Missionare erkennen. Auch ein Lügenmaul und ein Ärgermaul sind über dem Altar zu sehen, einfache Bilder, um die Grundwerte der neuen Religion zu veranschaulichen. Der engagierte Pastor weiß noch mehr Geschichten zu erzählen, auch aus der neueren Zeit, der braunen und der roten Invasionen.

If you lack the imagination to envision your inner swine, you had better go to Altenkirchen on the island of Rügen and visit the old church there, where you will find the beast painted on one of the walls. Those of you who have so often tried to drive it away will recognize it immediately.

There are many stories hidden in this old red brick church from around 1200 (one of the oldest churches in the entire Baltic Sea region). Built into the wall of a hidden chamber in the church, the so-called “Svantevit Stone” depicts a man blowing a horn. People who frequent Rügen may know that between 1068 and 1168, Jaromisburg, the biggest western Slavic Pagan sanctuary, dedicated to the four headed god Svantevit, stood at the island’s northern most point, the Kap Arkona. More than 300 temple servants watched over the temple’s treasure there. With its formidable location, the Slavs felt safe, not fearing any conquest of the temple. They were therefore all the more surprised when the Danes came by sea, attacking the sanctuary in 1163. The temple fell, and the Danes introduced Christianity. For the island’s inhabitants, the change in power was not all that dramatic. Instead of giving a tenth of their money to the high priest, they now had to give it to the bishop.

Built shortly after the invasion, the church at Altenkirchen somehow had to illustrate the change in religion. This was achieved with the help of symbols such as the inner swine. The wall painting depicts the frenzied pig running towards the church’s exit, symbolizing the drive outward of the new missionaries. These simple symbols were designed to explain the morals of the new religion. A lying mouth and an angry mouth are painted above the altar.

The priest who now looks after the church has many more stories to tell, especially when it comes to more recent history, with its brown (Nazi) and red (Communist) invasions.

So sieht er aus: der innere Schweinehund
This is how it looks: the Inner Swine

Amtsgebäude Altenkirchen
Lanckensburg 10
810556 Altenkirchen

p: 038391. 4010

f: 038391. 40144

Erntekrone: Die alten Traditionen werden wieder aufgegriffen
A Harvest Crown: the old traditions are coming back

Des Menschen bester Freund
Man's Best Friend

In der Stauferstadt Bad Wimpfen hütet eine Vegetarierin das einzige Glücksschweinemuseum der Welt. In acht Räumen wacht sie über ca. 10 000 Schweineexponate aus aller Welt, darunter Ritualmasken, mehrere Miss Piggys und eine Schweine-Peep-Show. Laut Museumswärterin stammt die Redewendung vom Glücksschwein aus dem 11. Jahrhundert. Damals gab es ein Ring-Werfe-Spiel, bei dem der Verlierer ein Schwein erhielt – angeblich eine Strafe, denn wohin mit dem Borstentier? Da sich die Schweine aber prächtig vom Dreck in den Straßen ernährten und dennoch rund und fett wurden und gar zu einer Mahlzeit taugten, wurde der Ausspruch „Schwein gehabt“ bald zur Redewendung.
Das Lieblingsexponat der Museumswärterin ist ein „Herr Völler“, ein Schwein, das eine Suppenterrine aus dem 19. Jahrhundert ziert. Diese gehörte einer Frau aus Mannheim, die die Terrine zu ihrer Hochzeit erhalten hatte. Das Schweinchen auf dem Deckel, so fand die Dame, sähe aus wie ein Metzger namens Völler und so nannte sie das Schweinchen „Herr Völler“. Im Zweiten Weltkrieg wurde ihr Haus bombardiert und alles ging zu Bruch – bis auf den Karton mit „Herrn Völler“. Als die Dame gestorben war, meinten ihre Erben, die Terrine gehöre ins Museum. Hier steht „Herr Völler“ nun inmitten all der anderen Schweine, von denen viele im Geheimen auch Namen haben, denn, so die Wärterin: „Manchmal gebe ich den Schweinen beim Katalogisieren Namen von Leuten, die ich nicht leiden kann. Das wird zwar kaum einer von denen erfahren, aber ich habe dabei eine große Genugtuung.“
Schwein gehabt, wenn man nicht darunter ist.

The "world's one and only" pig museum is being taken care of by a vegetarian. She is the curator of this 8-room museum with its 10,000 pigs from all over the world. Aside from the usual porcelain artifacts, there are ritual masks in the shape of pigs' heads, a couple of Miss Piggies, and a pig-peep-show.
In Germany, pigs have always played an important role. In addition to providing the country's most important sausage meat, and from being a swearword, the pig is also a symbol of good luck. This dates back to the 11th century when, in ring throwing games, the loser would win a farrow, ostensibly as a penalty: What were they supposed to do with the grimy beast? As the pig would then feast on the various filth which lay about the streets, getting fatter and fatter, the penalty actually turned out to be a blessing in disguise. That is where the German saying, Schwein gehabt comes from. This means, "I had pig!", or, "you had pig!" and is used to say that you have gotten lucky.
In the pig museum, the curator's favourite piece is named "Mr. Völler." Mr. Völler is a pig, which decorates an old porcelain soup tureen. This object belonged to a lady from nearby Mannheim. She had received the kitschy wonder as a wedding gift, and later noticed that the pig had a striking likeness to her butcher, a Mr. Völler (thus the name). During WWII, the lady's house was bombed, and everything was destroyed, except for an unpacked box that held Mr. Völler. After the lady died, her heirs decided to donate the pig tureen to the museum, which is where Mr. Völler is now, surrounded by other pigs, many of which have their own secret names. According to the curator, "When indexing our exhibits, I like to give names to some of the pigs, usually names of people who I don't like. Probably, nobody will ever even know about it, but it gives me a lot of satisfaction." If you are not among these eponyms, you have had pig!

Die Terrine mit Herrn Völler
The Mr. Völler tureen

Sammler- und Glückschwein-museum
Museum of Pigs
Kronengäßchen 2
74206 Bad Wimpfen

p: 07063. 6689

f: 07063. 6689

Öffnungszeiten:
täglich
10.00 – 17.00 Uhr

Opening hours:
daily
10 am – 5 pm

RELIGION und ARBEIT ist der
goldene Boden des Volkes

Tod in Deutschland

Death in Germany

Die Mumie des Ritters
The Knight's Mummy

Bei Kyritz, unweit nördlich vor den Toren Berlins, liegt der Leichnam des 1702 verstorbenen Ritters Christian Friedrich von Kahlbutz und will nicht verwesen. Warum ist bis heute auch nach etlichen Untersuchungen nicht geklärt. Er wurde weder vergiftet noch einbalsamiert. Jenseits der Wissenschaft weiß man besser Bescheid:
Kahlbutz forderte zu Lebzeiten gerne das „Recht der ersten Nacht" ein, wovon seine 11 ehelichen und an die 30 unehelichen Kinder zeugen. Dass dem cholerischen Ritter dieses Recht nicht immer gerne gewährt wurde, wird an der folgenden Geschichte deutlich und gilt als Grund seines jetzigen Zustands:
Ein Schäfer verweigerte ihm den Beischlaf mit seiner Frau und wurde kurz darauf tot aufgefunden. Zeugen hatten beobachtet, dass der Ritter eigenhändig den Schäfer niedergestreckt hatte. Der Ritter aber schwor vor Gericht, dass er es nicht gewesen sei und fügte freimütig hinzu: „Gott soll doch bitte verhindern, dass ich jemals die Erde verlasse, falls ich lüge."
Kahlbutz wurde freigesprochen und lebte noch etliche Jahre, bis er eines natürlichen Todes starb und in der Gruft der Kapelle zu Kyritz-Kampehl beigesetzt wurde. Zirka einhundert Jahre später wollte man dort die Särge umlagern und machte eine schauerliche Entdeckung: Alle Toten bis auf einen waren verwest. Ritter Kahlbutz lag wie eh und je in seinem Sarg. Man entsann sich des Schwurs von Kahlbutz vor Gericht, und bald rankten sich viele Gruselgeschichten um den Toten. Kahlbutz Schicksal wurde weltberühmt und der Besuch seiner Leiche wurde zu DDR-Zeiten ein beliebtes Ausflugsziel.
1936, während der Olympiade zu Berlin, boten Amerikaner und Japaner 250 000 Dollar für den Kauf der damals 300 Jahre alten Leiche von Ritter Kahlbutz.

Near Kyritz, just to the north of Berlin, the corpse of Knight Christian Friedrich of Kahlbutz has been lying around since 1702, and still has not decayed! After several scientific examinations, the phenomenon has still not been explained. What has been established, however, is that he had not been poisoned or embalmed. This mystery, it seems, must be solved by looking outside the world of science.
As a Knight, Kahlbutz was able to enjoy certain rights, among them, the ius primae noctis, or the "right to the first night." What this was can be surmised through learning that he had had 10 legitimate children, and 30 illegitimate. This right was not always granted willingly to our Knight. The following tale illustrates one such scenario:
A shepherd had refused allowing the Knight to sleep with his wife. Shortly thereafter, the man was mysteriously found dead in a field. Though eyewitnesses claimed to have seen the Knight murdering the poor shepherd, Kahlbutz swore on his innocence in court, under oath. Giving his Knight's word of honor, he added, "If I am lying, God shall prevent me from leaving this earth!"
The Knight of Kahlbutz was set free, and continued to lead a happy life until his death of natural causes at the age of 52. He was entombed in the vault at Kyritz-Kampehl and stayed there for about 100 years, until one day, when the vaults were rearranged, a chilling discovery was made. The corpses in the vault had all decayed, except for the Knight of Kahlbutz's! People then remembered his oath at court, and the news was quickly spread throughout the region.
Kahlbutz's story became world renowned, and in the former GDR, a visit to his corpse became a favorite among outings and excursions. During the 1936 Olympics in Berlin, American and Japanese businessmen offered up to $250,000 for the 300 years old Knight's corpse.

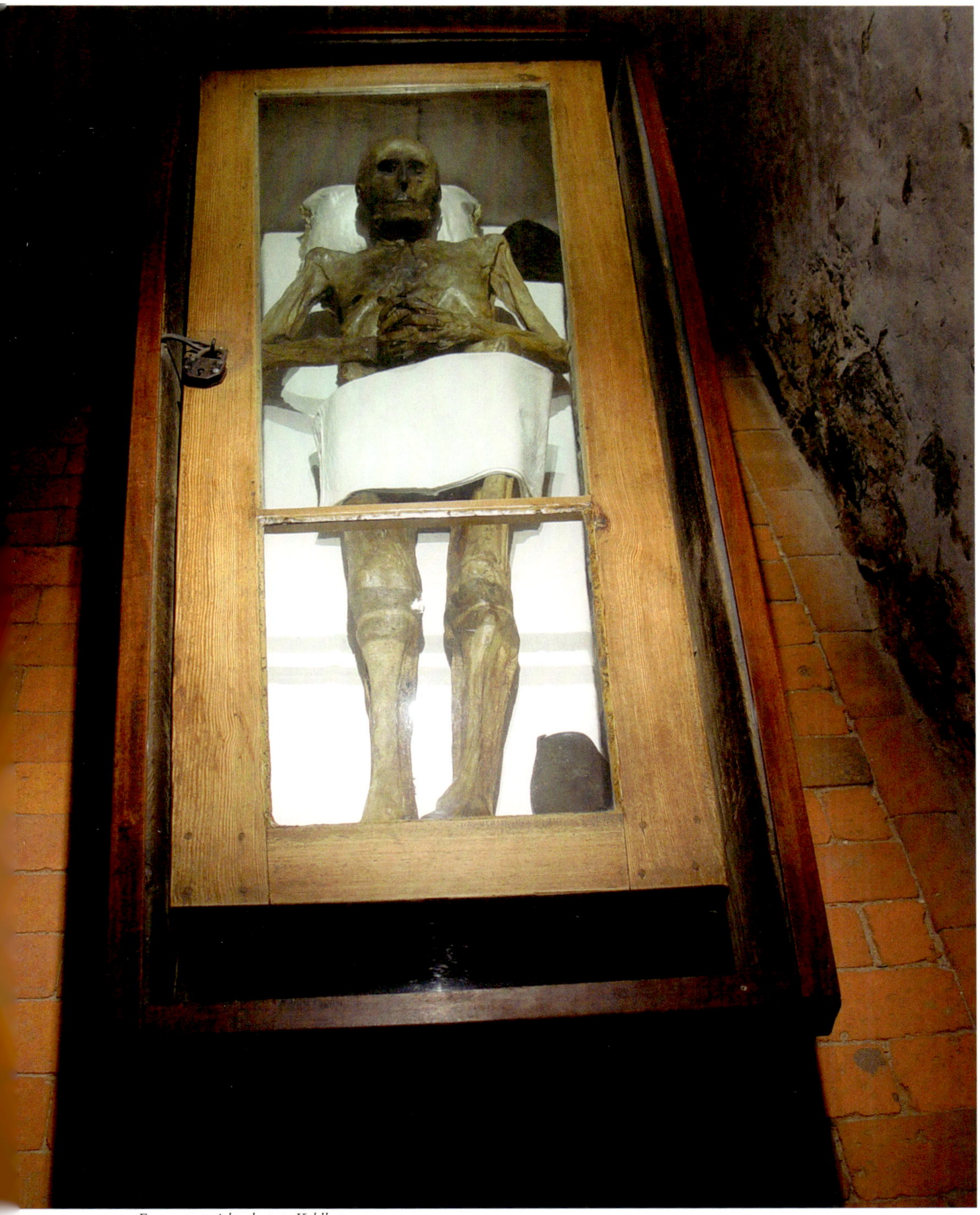

Der Ritter Kahlbutz
The Knight of Kahlbutz
Dorfkirche zu Kampehl
Village church of Kampehl
16845 Neustadt-Kampehl

p: 033970. 13405

www.kyritz.de/fvv/interessantes/kahlbutz.htm

Öffnungszeiten:
April bis Oktober:
Di bis So
10.00 – 12.00 und
13.00 – 17.00 Uhr
November bis März:
Di bis So
10.00 – 12.00 und
13.00 – 16.00 Uhr
Im Januar nur Samstag und Sonntag

Opening hours:
April to October:
Tue to Sun
10 am – 12 pm and
1 pm – 7 pm
November to March:
Tue to Sun
10 am – 12 pm and
1 pm – 4 pm
In January open on Sat and Sun only.

Er verrottet nicht: der tote Kahlbutz
He never decayed: the dead Kahlbutz

Rekonstruierte Kleidung eines Mannes aus dem 2. Jahrhunert nach Christus
Reconstructed clothing of a man from the second century after Christ

Moorleichen
Bog Bodies

Wer sich einmal Moorleichen ansehen will, tut dies am besten im Schloss Gottorf, im Schleswig-Holsteinischen Landesmuseum in Schleswig. Hier gibt es eine Vielzahl von Moorleichen, Hautschläuchen und Haarfrisuren – alles original aus der Zeit um 300 nach Christus, durch das Moor prächtig konserviert. Gefunden wurden die meisten Stücke durchs Torfstechen. Auch wenn die Moorleichen viel Aufschluss über das damalige Leben geben, weiß man heute noch immer nicht, warum die Leichen eigentlich im Moor lagen. Handelte es sich hierbei um ein Bestattungsritual, eine Strafe oder einen Opferritus?
Viele der Moorleichen wurden schon Ende des 19. Jahrhunderts gefunden. Beim Fund einer der Moorleichen fragte der Forscher beim lokalen Bäcker nach, ob der die Leiche nicht in seinem Backofen trocknen könne. Der Bäcker willigte ein: Gerne stellte er sich in den Dienst der Wissenschaft. Die Moorleiche überlebte, der Bäcker nicht. Niemand wollte mehr Brot aus seinem Ofen kaufen.
Ein anderes Ausstellungsstück im Museum ist ein Haufen Knochensplitter. Sie gehörten zu einer Frau, die vor achtzig Generationen in Norddeutschland gelebt hat. Geht man davon aus, dass sie in einer Zeit, der 200 Jahre Frieden folgten, gelebt hat, und dass sie wahrscheinlich fünf bis sechs

Anybody who might be interested in having a look at a bog body, a corpse which has been dug out of the moor, can do this best in Schloss Gottorf, in Schleswig Holsteinischen Landesmuseum in Schleswig. There are plenty of skin sheets and hairdos to be seen here – all originals, from the time period around 300 A.D. and wonderfully preserved through the moor. Most of the corpses were found as people were digging for peat. While these bog bodies give us many clues as to what life was like around 300 A.D., we still do not know why they ended up in the moor. Was it due to some kind of burial ritual, a civil punishment, or was it part of a sacrificial ritual?
Many of the moorland corpses were found back at the beginning of the last century. When one of these was discovered, a researcher asked at the local bakery if he could use the baker's oven to dry out the corpse. The baker consented: he would be more than happy to do his duty in service to science. The corpse "survived," but unfortunately, the baker did not. Nobody wanted to eat bread from his oven ever again.
Another attraction in the museum is a pile of bone splinters. These belonged to a woman who lived in northern Germany 80 generations ago. Knowing that she had lived in

Das Mädchen von Windeby
The girl from Windeby

Kinder hatte, kann man daraus schließen, dass sie ein Vorfahre der meisten Deutschen ist. Es gibt im Schloss Gottorf also nicht nur Moorleichen, sondern auch Ur-Ur-Ur-Großmütter zu bestaunen.

a time which was followed by 200 years of peace, and that she had probably had five to six children, we can surmise that she is an ancestor of almost every living German. Not only can you find bog bodies in Schloss Gottorf, but great great great great grandmothers as well.

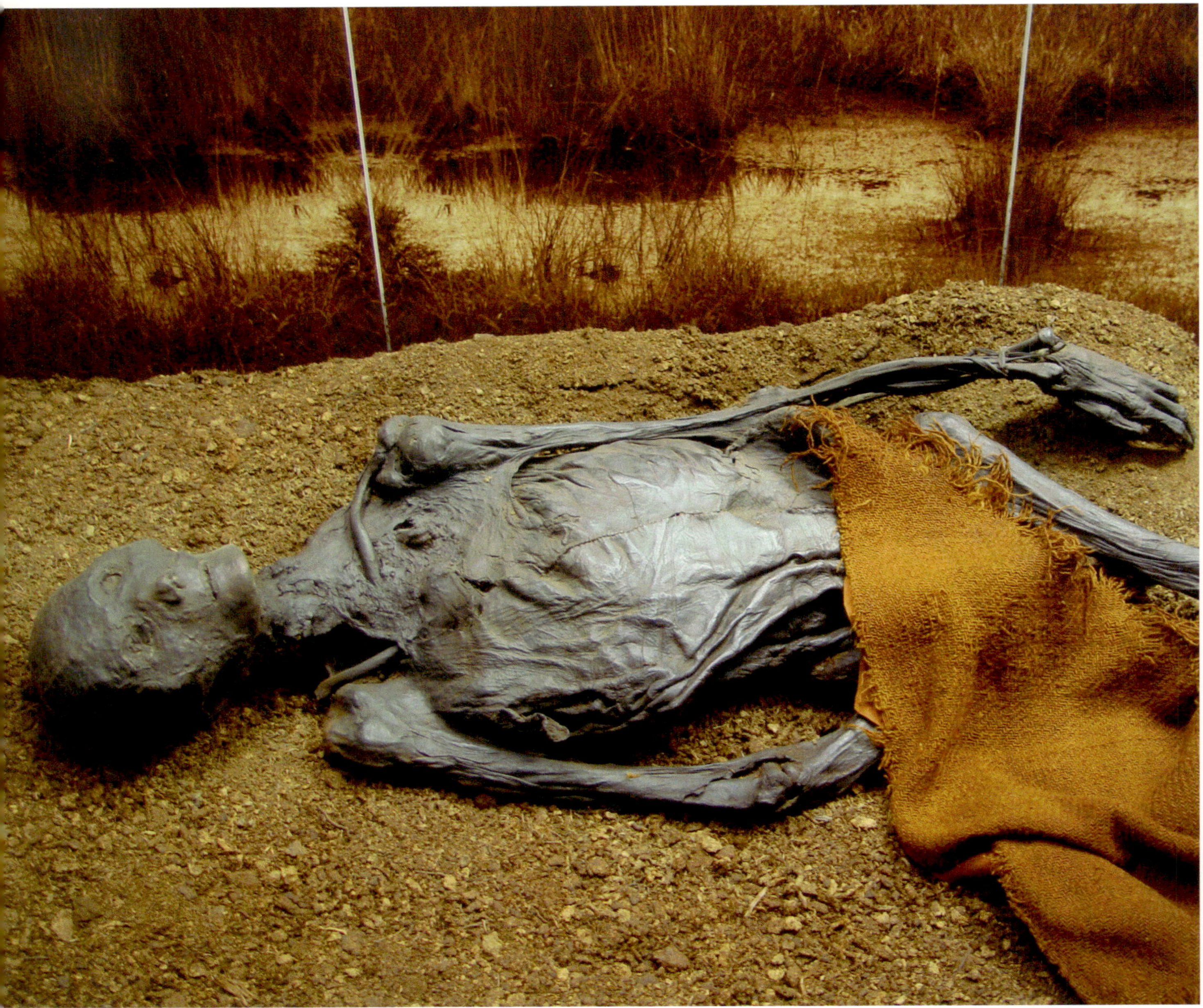

Der Mann von Rendswühren (gefunden 1871)
The man from Rendswühren (found in 1871)

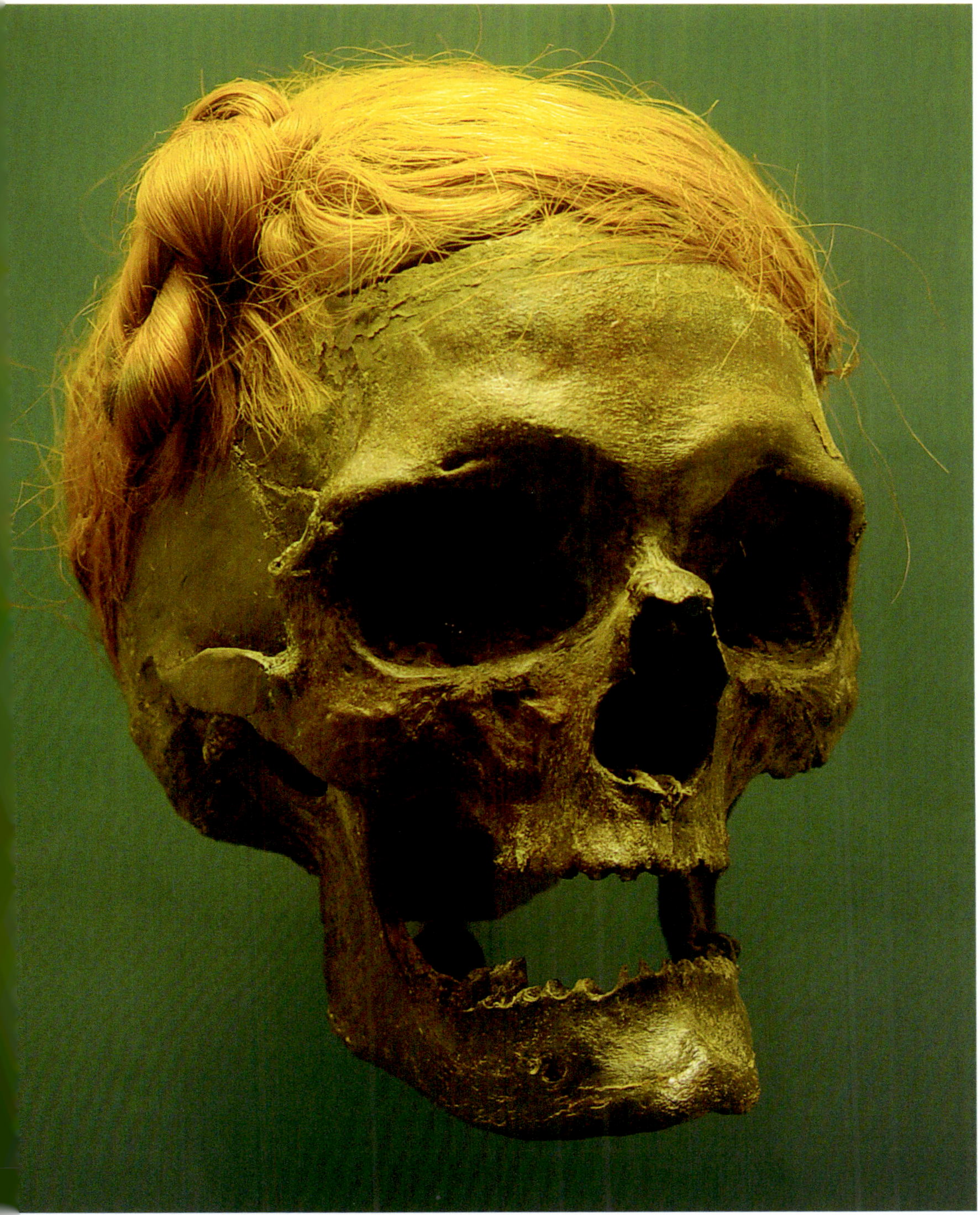

Stiftung Schleswig-Holsteinische Landesmuseen Schloss Gottorf
Schleswig Holstein State Museum Castle Gottorf
24837 Schleswig

p: 04621. 813300

f: 04621. 813535

www.schloss-gottorf.de

Öffnungszeiten:
April bis Oktober:
täglich
10.00 – 18.00 Uhr,
November bis März:
Di bis Fr
10.00 – 16.00 Uhr,
Sa und So
10.00 – 17.00 Uhr
(montags geschlossen)

Opening hours:
April to October:
daily
10 am – 6 pm
November to March:
Tue to Fri
10 am – 4 pm
Sat to Sun
10 am – 5 pm
(closed on Mondays)

Der Kopf von Osterby gehört zu einem Mann, der ca. 100 n. Christus gelebt hat
The head from Osterby belongs to a man who lived about 100 years after Christ

R.I.P. vs. RAF
A Resting Place for Terrorists

Der Dornhaldenfriedhof in Stuttgart-Degerloch ist ein Musterbeispiel schwäbischer Ordnungsliebe: Gleich am Eingang hängt die Friedhofsordnung, an jedem Brunnen stehen die Gießkannen in Reih und Glied, und Wege und Anlagen sind so sauber, dass man davon essen könnte.
Mitten in dieser spießigen Idylle liegen die drei gefährlichsten Terroristen der deutschen Nachkriegsgeschichte: Andreas Baader, Gudrun Ensslin und Jan Carl Raspe – die Führungsriege der Roten Armee Fraktion (RAF). Die gemeinsame Grabplatte sieht aus wie jede andere auch, polierter Stein, Standardschrift mit Serifen. Die Anlage hat den Charme einer Reihenhaussiedlung.
Dass Baader, Ensslin und Raspe hier beerdigt wurden, ist keine Selbstverständlichkeit. Ihr gemeinschaftlicher Selbstmord im Gefängnis Stuttgart-Stammheim entfachte Diskussionen auf Seiten der Linken und Rechten: Ein damals öffentlich diskutierter Vorschlag der Stammtischfraktionen war, die Leichen auf einer Müllhalde zu entsorgen. Der Stuttgarter Oberbürgermeister Manfred Rommel, Sohn des legendären „Wüstenfuchses“ griff persönlich in die Debatte um die Ruhestätte der Toten ein: Er wollte „sichtbar machen, dass mit dem Tod die Feindschaft endet“ und genehmigte die Bestattung auf dem Dornhaldenfriedhof.
Eine weitere Ironie der Geschichte: die RAF nahm ihre Motivation aus dem verdeckten Weiterbestehen von Nazi-Strukturen in der deutschen Gesellschaft. Der Friedhof in Degerloch ist auf dem ehemaligen Schießübungsplatz der Wehrmacht erbaut worden. Außerdem soll der Friedhof direkt nebenan, der Bergfriedhof, Hitlers Lieblingsfriedhof gewesen sein, wegen seiner „weihevollen Stille“.

The cemetery Dornhalde in Stuttgart-Degerloch can be seen as an excellent example of the Swabian love for order. Cemetery regulations are attached next to the entrance, watering cans are lined up in file, and the paths are clean enough to eat from.
Smack in the middle of this bourgeois landscape, the three most dangerous terrorists of German post-war history lay buried. The leaders of the left-wing terror group, RAF (Red Army Fraction), fought until death for a different Germany. Now, they lie silently in conformity, completely inconspicuous. Their graves look like any other in the cemetery: a polished stone inscribed with the standard serif font. One is reminded of a row of tract houses.
It was not a coincidence that Baader, Ensslin and Raspe were buried in this place. Their group suicide in the high security prison in nearby Stuttgart-Stammheim created a highly emotional discourse in Germany. It was publicly debated as to whether or not their corpses should be disposed of at a garbage dump. The Mayor of Stuttgart, Manfred Rommel, son of the “Desert Fox,” General Rommel, intervened in these discussions, making sure that the terrorists were buried in the cemetery at Dornhalden. He wanted to “make visible that enmity ends in death.”
Another irony of history: the members of the RAF were fighting against what they perceived to be a hidden continuity of Nazi structures in postwar Western German society. The place where they are buried used to be a firing range for the Nazi army. The nearby graveyard, Bergfriedhof, was Hitler’s favorite, due to its “solemn silence.”

Der saubere Dornhaldenfriedhof
The immaculate Dornhalden Cemetery

Dornhaldenfriedhof
Dornhalden Cemetery
Dornhalde 1 A
70597 Stuttgart

Das Grab von Baader, Ensslin und Raspe
Baader, Ensslin, and Raspes' grave

Drei Heilige in Bayern
Three Saints in Bavaria

Barocke Kirchen in Bayern beherbergen oft ungewöhnliche schlummernde Bewohner: In einer Nische im Kirchenschiff findet sich ein echtes menschliches Skelett, aufgebahrt in einem gläsernen Sarg mit Goldornamenten. Manchmal an einem Glas Wein nippend, manchmal einfach so in die Gemeinde blickend sind solche Skelette mit Borden, Ringen und Kronen geschmückt. In den Augenhöhlen stecken dann gerne Glasmurmeln, oder die Augen werden einfach auf ein Papier aufgemalt.

Katakombenheilige nennt man solche Gesellen und sie gehen auf eine Zeit zurück, in der jede Kirchengemeinde, die etwas auf sich hielt, eine Reliquie haben musste. Nur haben die Hauptheiligen eine begrenzte Anzahl von Knochen und wenn diese alle vergeben sind, muss man sich etwas anderes einfallen lassen. So fing man im bayrischen Barock an, Skelette aus den Katakomben von Rom zu importieren – man wusste um die Märtyrer dort, und diese mussten sicherlich heilig sein. In richtigen Prozessionen wurden die Gebeine von Unbekannten in bayrische Kirchen überbracht und mit lateinischen Namen versehen.

In Rott am Inn liegen zwei solcher Katakombenheiligen, Marinus und Anianus. Man hat in der prächtigen Kirche allerdings Glück gehabt und hat am Ende des 20. Jahrhunderts doch noch einen Heiligen, zumindest für die Bayern, abbekommen: In einer Gruft am Rande des Friedhofs ist Franz Josef Strauß beigesetzt worden.

Many of the baroque churches in Bavaria house eccentric guests. It is not unusual at all for human skeletons to be found relaxing in some niche in the nave of the church. They are usually laid out in ostentatiously decorated glass coffins (good old Baroque!), and their bones are adorned with golden ornaments, rings and crowns. These rather quiet tenants are often seen holding wine goblets or bibles in their bony hands. Other times, they just stare intently out into the congregation; their staring eyes either painted onto the skull, or made of special marbles which have been carefully placed into the eye sockets.

These skeletons are called "catacomb saints," and date back to the time when churches were collecting relics in order to attract an audience. As real relics were limited and had already been well distributed amongst the big and wealthy cathedrals, smaller and younger churches had to look for alternatives. They began importing corpses from the catacombs in Rome, declaring them to be holy. The chances were high, after all, that a Roman corpse of this sort had been a Christian martyr. The skeletons were given Latin names in big processions, and were then transferred to their new homes in Bavaria.

In the baroque church at Rott am Inn, two such catacomb saints are slumbering; one named Marinus, and the other, Anianus. This pompous church, however, was lucky and even got hold of a real saint at the end of the 20th century. This was none other than the former Bavarian Prime Minister Franz Josef Strauß, a very conservative and highly controversial politician of the time. Many old-school Bavarians do in fact speak of this man in saintly terms. For the younger generations, Strauß has been much less popular. He can in any rate now be found resting in a tomb at the edge of the church's cemetery.

Ein Katakombenheiliger
A holy catacomber

Gruft von Franz Josef Strauß
The tomb of Franz Josef Strauß

Klosterkirche
Cloister Church
Kaiserhof 3
83543 Rott am Inn

p: 08039. 90680

e: info@rottinn.de

www.rottinn.de

Heimatstätte für Heimatlose

A Home for the Homeless

Sylt zieht nicht nur Deutschlands Urlauber an, sondern auch die Leichen von Schiffbrüchigen. In solchen Fällen wird der Strandinspektor gerufen, der diese dann an den Küster weitergibt, der für ein ordentliches Begräbnis sorgt. 1854 war ein gewisser Wulf Hansen Strandinspektor, der beschloss für die unbekannten Seeleute einen eigenen Friedhof zu öffnen, eine Heimatstätte für Heimatlose. So hieß der Friedhof dann auch und wurde zur letzten Heimat für 53 Seeleute, die zwischen 1854 und 1907 am Westerländer, Rantumer und Hörnumer Strand gefunden wurden.

Einfache Holzkreuze versehen mit Datum und Fundort stehen hier in Reih und Glied, Rosen und Zierrasen tun ihre Pflicht. Königin Elisabeth von Rumänien spendete 1888 einen Gedenkstein, auf dem eine Strophe des Liedes „Heimat für Heimatlose“ eingraviert ist. Wie sie dazu kam, bleibt ungewiss, reichte aber dafür aus, die Straße, an der der Friedhof heute liegt, Elisabethenstraße zu nennen. Diese führt durch eine Neubausiedlung.

Man findet den Friedhof am besten, wenn man die Einkaufstraße von Westerland Richtung Strand läuft und dann bei McDonalds links abbiegt.

Not only does Sylt attract holidaymakers from throughout Germany; the North Sea island attracts shipwrecked corpses as well. In such cases, the beach inspector is called in to assess the situation, after which the parish clerk is notified, who then arranges for a decent burial. In 1884, a certain Wulf Hansen, beach inspector, decided to open up a cemetery for the unknown seamen and women. It was called a "Heimatstätte für Heimatlose," or "A Home for the Homeless," and became exactly that for the 53 seafarers who were found on the beaches of Sylt between 1854 and 1907.

The cemetery is lined with simple wood crosses, each of which is furnished with the date and place of the unfortunate discovery. A nicely mowed lawn and rows of roses serve to add a bit of greenery and color. Queen Elisabeth of Romania donated a memorial stone in which a verse from the song, "Home for the Homeless," is engraved. How she came to this decision, we will never know, but that she did, was enough to have had the street which leads to the cemetery named Elisabethenstraße. The street leads right through a block of modern housing units.

The cemetery can most easily be found by walking down Westerland's shopping street towards the beach, and then turning left at McDonalds.

Heimatstätte für Heimatlose
Elisabethenstraße
25980 Westerland

Hier finden angeschwemmte Leichen ihre letzte Ruhe
This is where shipwrecked corpses find a last place of rest

Blut an der Unterhose
Bloody Underpants

In Ansbach kann man die blutverschmierte Unterhose des geheimnisvollen Kaspar Hauser bestaunen. Alle paar Jahre versuchen Genforscher an Hand der Blutflecken das Geheimnis um Kaspar Hauser zu lösen.
Tatsache ist, dass Kaspar 1828 als ca. 16 jähriger in Nürnberg auftauchte. Er konnte nicht sprechen und benahm sich „pudelnärrisch" – wie Zeugen zu Protokoll gaben. Beim Verhöhr war der junge Mann auch nicht sehr hilfreich – nur seinen Namen konnte er mühsam, aber leserlich niederschreiben. Ansonsten stellte er sich tolpatschig an. Man nahm an, dass der Junge sein Leben lang in Gefangenschaft zugebracht haben musste.
Er erhielt einen Pflegevater und Mentor, lernte Sprechen, Schreiben und Lesen und zeigte eine hohe musische Begabung. Doch 1829 wurde diese positive Entwicklung unterbrochen: Ein Unbekannter versuchte, ihn auf der Toilette umzubringen. Der Anschlag machte aus dem Lokalfall Hauser eine europäische Berühmtheit. Sowohl der bayrische König als auch ein mysteriöser Gönner aus England zeigten Interesse an Kaspar Hauser. Zwei Theorien durchwanderten die höfische Gesellschaft: Manche sahen Kaspar als genialen Hochstapler, andere als zu Unrecht dem Thron erhobenen Erbprinzen von Baden, der eventuell oder sogar mit Napoleon verwandt sei.
Nach dem ersten Attentat zog Kaspar Hauser nach Ansbach und arbeitete am Appellationsgericht. Zwei Jahre später wurde Kaspar im Winter auf einem Spaziergang durch den Ansbacher Hofgarten wieder angegriffen – diesmal überlebte er den Anschlag nicht. Er konnte sich durch Schneegestöber noch nach Hause schleppen und berichtete von einem Treffen mit einem Unbekannten, der ihm seine Herkunft verraten wollte. Man fand am Tatort einen Zettel in Spiegelschrift – der liegt jetzt im Museum von Ansbach zusammen mit der blutigen Unterhose. Im Hofgarten wurde ein Gedenkstein aufgestellt: „HIC OCCULTUS OCCULTO OCCISUS EST" – Hier wurde ein Unbekannter von einem Unbekannten ermordet.

The mysterious Kaspar Hauser's bloody underpants are out on display in the town of Ansbach. Every so often, researchers bring out the latest technology in an attempt, which has so far been fruitless, to solve the mystery of Kaspar Hauser.
Hauser appeared in Nuremberg in 1828 at the approximate age of 16. He was not able to talk, and according to witnesses, behaved like a "mad poodle." Though an interrogation did not lead to many useful conclusions, he was able to write his name, if barely legible. He behaved clumsily and did strange things. It was thus assumed that Kaspar Hauser had grown up in complete imprisonment. He was then taken into care by a foster father who taught him how to speak, read, and write. In addition to this, he showed a great talent for drawing and for playing the piano.
These positive developments came to an end when in 1829; somebody tried to kill Kaspar Hauser while he was sitting on a toilet. The attempted murder made the young man's case famous throughout Europe, and the king of Bavaria as well as a mysterious benefactor in England began to show interest in Hauser's plight. Two theories were developed among the European aristocracy. Some believed that Kaspar Hauser was actually the inheritor of the Lord of Baden, which would have made him a relative of Napoleon. Others thought that he was just an incredibly gifted imposter.
Hauser moved to the small town of Ansbach where he started working at the local court. Two years later, there was a second attempt on his life, and this time, unfortunately, it was a successful one. Kasper Hauser was killed in the winter by an unknown assailant while walking through the Ansbach Hofgarten (palace gardens). He was able to make it home despite his wounds, and before dying, told of a meeting with a man who was to reveal to him the secrets of his origin. The bloody underpants on display in the museum are the ones he was wearing on this fatal day. In the Hofgarten, a memorial stands in honor of Kaspar Hauser. It reads: HIC OCCULTUS OCCULTO OCCISUS EST – An Unknown has been Killed Here by an Unknown.

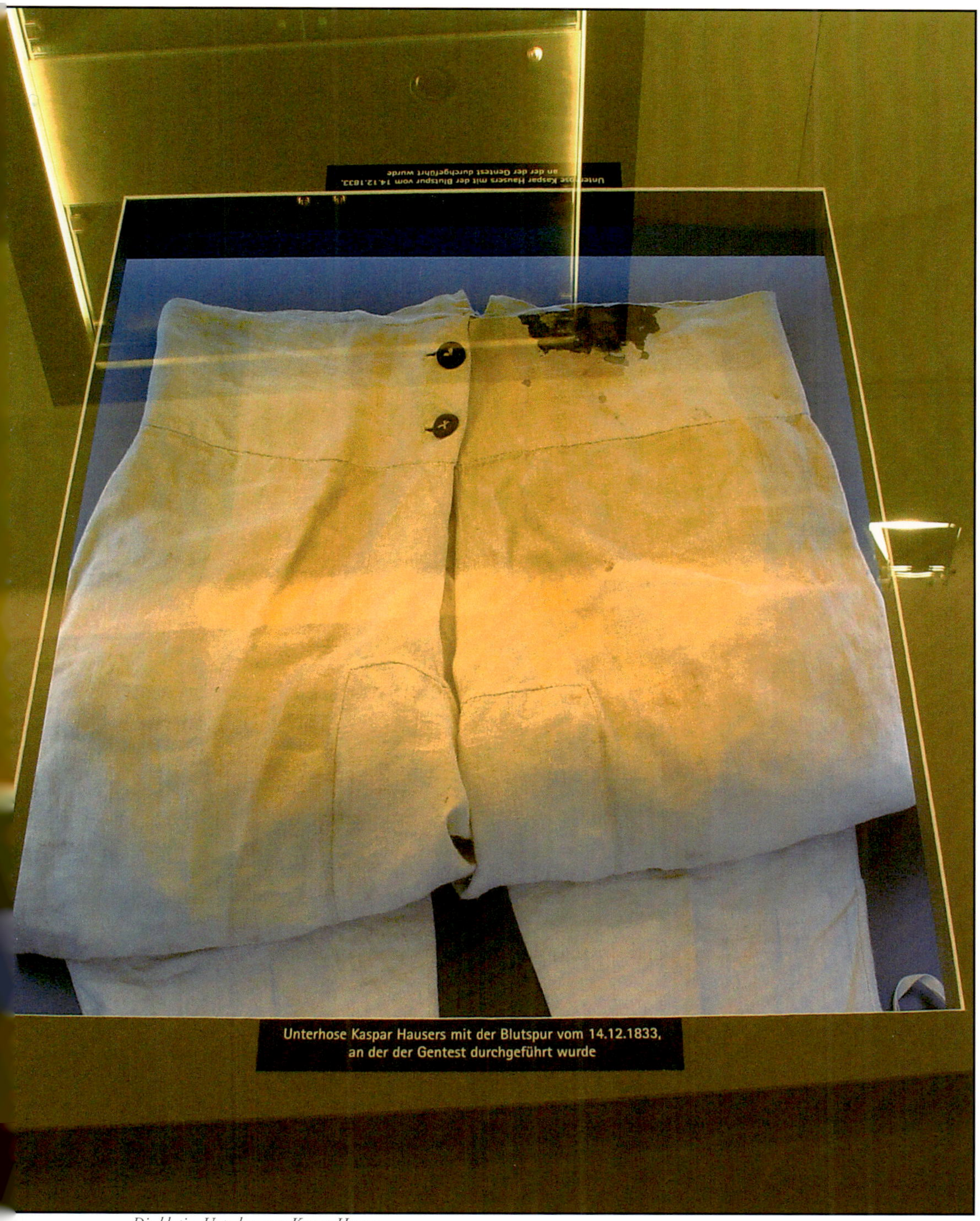

Die blutige Unterhose von Kaspar Hauser
Kaspar Hauser's bloody underpants

Kaspar-Hauser-Ausstellung
Kaspar Hauser Exhibition
Markgrafenmuseum
Kaspar-Hauser-Platz 1
91522 Stadt Ansbach

p: 0981. 9775056

Öffnungszeiten:
März bis Oktober:
täglich
10.00 – 16.00 Uhr
November bis Februar:
täglich außer Montag
10.00 – 16.00 Uhr

Opening hours:
March to October:
daily
10 am – 4 pm
November to February:
Every day but Monday
10 am – 4 pm

Kaspar-Hauser-Denkmal
Kaspar Hauser Memorial
Platenstraße
91522 Stadt Ansbach

Bäume für die Toten
Trees for the Dead

Der Friedwald im Rheinhardswald (siehe auch Seite 52/53) ist der älteste Friedwald in Deutschland – er wurde am 7. November 2001 eingeweiht. Ein Friedwald ist ein neues Bestattungskonzept, dessen Ursprungsidee aus der Schweiz stammt: Anstatt in einem wuchtigen Grab auf einem Friedhof beigesetzt zu werden, erwirbt man sich in einem eigens dafür vorgesehenen Wald einen Baum. Nach dem Tod wird die Asche unter den Wurzeln des Baumes vergraben.

Wenn so gewünscht, wird der Baum mit einer einfachen Plakette versehen – nur die Lebensdaten und der Name stehen darauf. So ist der Baum Grab und Grabmahl in einem. Die Grabpflege wird von der Natur übernommen. Auch fallen Friedhofsgebühren und Grabverlängerungen weg – mit einem Baum im Friedwald verbündet man sich für 99 Jahre. Von außen ist der Wald nicht als Begräbnisplatz erkennbar. Die Angehörigen erhalten eine Waldkarte, auf der der Baum eingezeichnet ist. Der Besuch des Grabes lässt sich so mit einem Waldspaziergang verbinden – so findet der Besucher vielleicht die nötige Ruhe, um in Erinnerungen zu verweilen.

Der Verein Friedwald e.V. vergibt alte und neue Bäume, die man sich schon zu Lebzeiten aussuchen kann. Seit seiner Gründung konnte der Verein Friedwald in Deutschland zwei weitere Friedwälder „ins Leben rufen". In der Schweiz gibt es sogar schon 27 Friedwälder.

The Friedwald, or Peace Forest, in Rheinhardswald (see page 52/53) is the oldest of its kind in Germany, founded in November 2001. Originating in Switzerland, a Peace Forest is an innovative funeral concept. Instead of heavy gravestones and mausoleums, the family buys a tree in the Peace Forest, under which, the ashes of the deceased are buried.

In place of a stone engraving, the "owner" of the tree is memorialized by a small plaque with only their name on it, dates of birth and death being given only when requested. After buying the tree, there are no additional costs, the job of maintenance being taken over by nature, and the deceased are connected to their trees for the next 99 years. The idea behind the forest, which is not recognizable as a cemetery from the outside, is to leave human intervention out, letting nature take its course.

Relatives receive a map on which their tree is highlighted. Visiting the grave means taking a peaceful walk through the woods, having time and quiet to think of the beloved and departed.

The association Friedwald ev. offers both new and old trees, and people usually select their own tree during their lifetime. Since this first Peace Forest was established in Germany, two others have been opened. In Switzerland, there are already 27 of these peaceful places of rest.

Friedwald im Reinhardswald
34369 Hofgeismar

Friedwald Deutschland e.V.
Flotowstrasse 9
64289 Darmstadt

p: 06151. 7347580 oder/ or
0700.FRIEDWALD

www.friedwald.de

Schlichte Plaketten statt schwerer Grabplatten
Sleek plaques instead of heavy engraving

Der Sarg der Königin Louise von Preußen

The Coffin of Queen Louise from Prussia

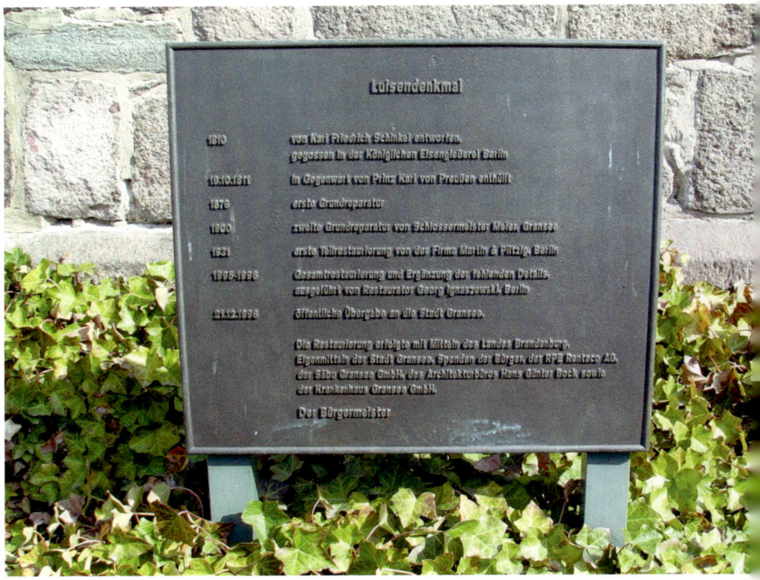

In manchen Gegenden Deutschlands passiert Jahrhunderte lang reichlich wenig von historischer Bedeutung. So auch in der kleinen Kreisstadt Gransee in der Uckermark, ca. 80 km nördlich von Berlin. Nur einmal geschah hier etwas wirklich Außergewöhnliches, etwas so Bedeutsames, dass die Bürger Gransees ein ganzes Jahr lang Geld gesammelt und davon ein Denkmal errichtet haben.

In der Nacht vom 25. auf den 26. Juli 1810 weilte der Leichnam der Königin Louise von Preußen auf dem Marktplatz von Gransee. Sie war in Hohenzieritz – nicht weit von Gransee – während eines Besuches in der Sommerresidenz ihres Vaters verstorben und sollte nun nach Berlin überführt werden. Der Trauerzug bewegte sich nur langsam weiter und kam am Abend des 25. Juli in Gransee an. Die Totenwächter ließen sich einquartieren, die tote Königin wurde auf dem Marktplatz aufgebahrt, die Bürger waren begeistert. Königin Louise von Preußen, in ihrer Stadt – endlich passierte hier ein historisches Ereignis.

Etwas mehr als ein Jahr darauf, am 9. Oktober 1811, konnte das Denkmal auf dem Marktplatz eingeweiht werden: ein Sarg mit einer goldenen Krone und einem viktorianischen Baldachin, dazu ein paar Gedenktafeln in Gold. Leider konnte der König selbst nicht kommen, doch der

In some regions of Germany, centuries pass by without anything at all of historical importance happening. This has been the case in the small town of Gransee in the county Uckermark, about 80 km north of Berlin. There was one time though, when something really "big" happened here. The event was so big, in fact, that the citizens of Gransee spent a whole year collecting money in order to build a monument in its honor.

On the night of the 25th and 26th of July 1810, the body of Queen Louise of Prussia was carried through the town of Gransee. She had died at her father's summer residence in Hohenzyritz, not far from Gransee. Her corpse needed to be transferred to Berlin, and advancing very slowly, the funeral procession arrived in Gransee on the evening of the 25th of July. Members of the funeral procession checked into the local inn, and the dead Queen was laid out on display in the local market square. The citizens were enthusiastic. Imagine, the Queen of Prussia, there in their own market place – finally something BIG was happening!

After roughly one year, on October the 9th, 1811, the inauguration of the memorial to this event could finally take place. A Victorian canopy and a coffin topped with a golden crown were brought into the market square, and a

Hier stand einst der Sarg von Königin Louise, jetzt steht hier ein Denkmal
Here once stood Queen Louise's coffin; now there is a monument in its place

junge 10-jährige Kronprinz reiste zur feierlichen Eröffnung an. Auch heute noch ist man in Gransee stolz auf die Königin und das Denkmal. Es ist herrlich restauriert, und im Stadtmuseum findet man noch die alten schwarzen Tücher, die damals den Sarg zierten.

description of the bizarre monument was engraved in golden letters. Unfortunately, the King himself was unable to attend the opening ceremony, but in his place, the 10-year-old crown prince was there to enjoy the festivities.
The people of Gransee are still very proud of their memorial and of "their" Queen. The monument has just recently been lavishly restored. The black draperies that were used to decorate the Queen's coffin are on display in the local museum.

Inschrift auf dem Denkmal:
geb. d. 10 März 1776
gest. d. 19 Juli 1810
nachts d. 25. Juli 1810
stand ihre Leiche hier

Inscription on the monument:
born on March 10th 1776
died on July 19th 1810
in the night of July 25th 1810
her corpse once stood here

Touristen-Information
Rudolf-Breitscheid-Str. 44
16775 Gransee

p: 03306. 21606

www.gransee-info.de

Siegfriedbrunnen Odenheim
Siegfried Springs at Odenheim

Siegfried von Xanten aus der Nibelungensage wurde durch Hagen von Tronje an einer Quelle ermordet. Seither streiten sich mindestens fünf deutsche Orte, Standort der wahren Siegfriedquelle zu sein. So auch das Dorf Odenheim im Kraichgau mit seinem Siegfriedbrunnen. Der Anspruch des Dorfes darf ernst genommen werden: Laut Dorfchronik hieß Odenheim früher Wotanhain und war Opferplatz für Wotan. Der Brunnen, aus dem die angebliche Siegfriedquelle tritt, liegt mitten im Wald: einst führte eine Römerstraße hier entlang. Alt ist der Ort! Das fand auch ein zu Anfang des 20. Jahrhunderts nach Amerika ausgewanderter Odenheimer und stiftete einen Gedenkstein, der die Echtheit der Quelle bezeugen soll.

Einen Haken hat die Sache mit der Quelle: Obwohl die Odenheimer um sie herum einen Picknickplatz errichtet haben, steht hier ein Warnschild: das Wasser ist nicht auf Trinkbarkeit geprüft. Das scheint ihrer Beliebtheit nicht zu schaden. Eine Gruppe Zigeuner füllt das Quellwasser in mitgebrachte Kanister. Auf die Frage, warum, folgt ein Schulterzucken und „machen wir schon immer so". Dann gibt es noch einen Mann, der hier Wasser für seine Schnapsbrennerei holt – er schwört auf den reinen Geschmack der Quelle. Sein Vater und Großvater hätten das auch so gemacht. Auch eine Frau kommt mit dem Auto vorbeigefahren, um sich nach einem Tag auf der Arbeit im Rinnsal der Quelle die Füße zu kühlen.

Siegfried von Xanten, from the Nibelungen Saga, was murdered by Hagen von Tronje at a well. Since then, at least five German towns have been fighting about which town can claim to be the authentic location of the event. One of these is the village of Odenheim in Kraichgau, with its Siegfried Springs. The town's assertions can be taken somewhat seriously: According to the village chronicles, Odenheim used to be called Wotanheim and was the place of sacrifice to Wotan, the highest Germanic god. The well from which the alleged Siegfried Springs flows lies in the middle of a forest, through which a Roman street once led. This is an old village! Having this in mind, a citizen of Odenheim, who had immigrated to America at the beginning of the 20th century, decided to endow the place with a memorial stone, which is supposed to testify to the authenticity of the springs.

There is just one catch with the springs. Although the citizens of Odenheim have built up a picnic park around it, there is a warning sign at the well: "This water has not been approved for drinking!" This however does not seem to detract from its endearment. During our visit, a group of gypsies filled their canisters full with the famous water. In response to our asking why, we got a shrug of the shoulders and, "That's how we've always done it." A man who always gets his water here for his Schnapps distillery swears by the clean taste of the spring's water. His father, and his father before that, had also always done it like that. A woman then drove by, stopping after a long day's work in order to cool her feet in the rill of the spring's well.

Ein nach Amerika ausgewanderter Odenheimer spendete die Einfassung der Quelle
An American immigrant from Odenheim paid for the mounting of the spring

76684 Odenheim

Braune Spuren

Brown Traces

Modell von Hitlers Haus, dem Berghof, in Berchtesgaden
Model of the Berghof, Hitler's house in Berchtesgaden

Das Adlernest
The Eagle's Nest

Berchtesgaden lebt von der schönen Bergwelt um den Watzmann und den letzten Spuren seiner braunen Vergangenheit. Denn hier auf dem Obersalzberg ließ Hitler seine Sommerresidenz errichten, mit allem, was für einen Staatsmann dazugehört: Kasernen, Hotels, Verwaltungsgebäuden und Villen für die Nazi-Prominenz.
Und diese braune Vergangenheit beschert den Berchtesgadenern in der Tat eine ergiebige Geldquelle: Um sich mal ein Stück „echten Bunker" im unfreundlichen „Hotel zum Türken" anzuschauen, zahlt man den gleichen Preis wie anderswo für die Geisterbahn, sieht aber weit weniger. Für die Fahrt zum legendären „Eagle's nest", dem Teehaus Hitlers auf dem Kehlstein, muss man nicht nur die 120 Meter lange Aufzugsfahrt zahlen, sondern auch den Bus dorthin und den Parkplatz vor dem Bus – alles natürlich weit überteuert.
Ganz angenehm ist da eine kleine Kamera-Audio-Box an der Bushaltestelle. Dieses funktionstüchtige, mittlerweile antiquierte Kästchen zeigt anhand von kolorierten Dias und einem vorgetragenem Begleittext, was einen auf dem Kehlstein und der Fahrt dorthin erwartet. Danach muss man gar nicht mehr selbst hinfahren, sondern hat für nur 20 Cent alles gesehen. Vielleicht ein Überbleibsel aus der

The people of Berchtesgaden live off of the lovely scenery of the city's surrounding mountains, and from the traces of its Nazi history. It is here in the picturesque setting of Obersalzberg, where Hitler had his second headquarters: a huge complex of barracks, offices, officer's housing units, and hotels.
This little piece of "brown history" (in Germany, the color brown is often associated with the Nazis, partly because of the brown shirts which were part of their uniforms) has created a substantial stream of capital for the citizens of Berchtesgaden: Tourists wanting to see the "real bunker" beneath the unfriendly Hotel zum Türken will be disappointed to learn that the tunnel of horrors at their local carnival would have been much cheaper and, for that matter, more interesting as well.
For the trip up to the legendary "Eagle's Nest," Hitler's tea house at the top of Mount Kehlstein, visitors will not only have to pay for the bus ride up, but when they arrive, will have to pay for a 120 meter high elevator ride as well. If you would like to go by car, you will, of course, have to pay a parking fee. Needless to say, the rates are overpriced.
One nice thing in Berchtesgaden is the little photo-audio box which we found at the bus stop on the way up to the

Sechs der zehn Stereofarbdias, die die Fahrt zum Kehlsteinhaus dokumentieren
Six out of the ten techno-color-slides, which illustrate the trip up to the Eagle's Nest

Zeit, in der Hitler öfter nach Berchtesgaden kam: Wenn der Führer zu Besuch war, durften die Kinder jeden Samstag um 14 Uhr kostenlos ins Kino.

tea house. The outmoded but still functioning machine shows highlights of the Eagle's Nest and its surrounding scenery on hand-colored slides. An inspired pre-recorded male voice adds commentary to the slightly faded pictures. After seeing and hearing the program for 20 cents, there is no need to go any further: You have seen it all. Perhaps this cute little service dates back to the time when Hitler used to come to Berchtesgaden: During the Führer's stay in town, kids were invited to go to the cinema on Saturday afternoons – for free!

Automaten aus längst vergangener Zeit
Automats from a bygone era

Weitere Stereofarbdias aus Berchtesgaden
More techno-color slides from Berchtesgaden

Kehlsteinhaus
The Eagle's Nest
83471 Berchtesgaden

p: 08652. 2969

e: eder-berchtesgaden@ t-online.de

www.eagles-nest.de

Öffnungszeiten:
Mai bis Oktober: geöffnet
November bis April: geschlossen

Opening times:
May to October: open
November to April: closed

Die arischen Truthähne

The Aryan Turkeys

Wie war es möglich, dass ausgerechnet die größte Entdeckung der Seefahrt, die Entdeckung Amerikas, dem Juden Christoph Columbus zu verdanken sei? Für die Nazis ein Unding. Und so waren sie verständlicherweise sehr dankbar, als Kunsthistoriker im Dom zu Schleswig eine ungewöhnliche Entdeckung machten: Im Kreuzgang wurden Wandmalereien gefunden, die eindeutig Truthähne zeigen. Und das in einem Gebäude, das um 1280 erbaut wurde – knapp 250 Jahre vor der vermeindlichen Entdeckung Amerikas durch Christoph Columbus. Und da Truthähne als uramerikanische Tiere galten, war schnell klar, wer wirklich diesen Kontinent entdeckt hatte: die ur-arischen Wikinger!

Erst in den 50er Jahren stellte sich heraus, dass sich die Sache mit den Truthähnen ganz anders verhielt: Die Wandmalerei stammt nicht aus der Zeit der Erbauung der Kathedrale, sondern von einem gewissen Hans Olbers, der in den Jahren 1887–1894 den Auftrag hatte, den Kreuzgang zu renovieren und – wo nötig – zu ergänzen. Er hielt Truthähne wohl für ein adäquates Motiv, das gut zu den anderen biblischen Geschichten passte. Außerdem fand man heraus, dass bei einer Restauration von 1933–1940 der Auftragnehmer Lothar Malskat nicht nur die Zahl der Truthähne verdoppelt, sondern auch neue Porträtköpfe im Bogen des östlichen Chorfensters einfügte – aus 13 wurden 26. Bei den neuen Köpfen standen unter anderem der Vater des Restaurators, der Domküster und die Filmschauspielerin Hansi Knoteck Modell. Maskats künstlerische Bearbeitung war damit noch lange nicht zu Ende: Auf der Rückseite eines der Grabmäler porträtierte er sich selbst eine Zigarette rauchend. Heute ist dieser Bereich leider nicht mehr zugänglich für die Besucher.

Als man den Betrug aufdeckte, wurde Malskat zu 20 Monaten Gefängnis bestraft. Im Lübecker Dom hatte er auch im Zuge von Restaurationsarbeiten einige Eigenkreationen mit eingeschmuggelt, diese wurden aber im Gegensatz zu Schleswig sofort ausgebessert.

How could it be that the Jew, Christopher Columbus, had been responsible for one of the most important discoveries in the history of sea travel: the discovery of America? This quandary was a nightmare for the Nazis. They were therefore relieved when art historians made an interesting discovery in the cathedral of Schleswig in Northern Germany: Mural paintings, clearly depicting turkeys, were found in the cloister, which had been built in 1280, nearly 250 years before Columbus had discovered America. Turkeys being the American bird par excellence, it was rashly deduced that not Columbus, but the Aryan Vikings must have discovered America.

In the 1950's, it was revealed that the whole story with the turkeys had not been completely accurate: The mural paintings were found not to be from the time of the cathedral's construction, but had instead been painted in by a man named Hans Olbers during a restoration between the years 1887 and 1894. He had apparently decided that the turkeys would make a superb complement to the biblical symbols painted there. Amusingly, that was not all. In a later restoration from 1933–1940, a Lothar Malskat had found the turkeys to be so charming that he decided to double their number! A couple of other changes were also made by Malskat: 13 new portraits were added to the choir, some of them looking very similar to a few of the artist's friends. The artist's father, the actress Hansi Knoteck, and the cathedral's sexton, can all be clearly recognized in the mural. Malskat, employing a bit of artistic freedom, then went a step further, painting a portrait of himself smoking a cigarette on the back of a tomb in the cathedral. Unfortunately, access to this part of the church is no longer given to the public. When the fraud was discovered, the artist was punished with 20 months imprisonment. It was later learned that he had also decorated the cathedral in nearby Lübeck with his creations. These were promptly removed.

St. Petri Dom zu Schleswig
St. Petri's dome in Schleswig

Truthahn (Detail)
Turkey (detail)

St. Petri Dom
St. Petri's Cathedral
Norderdomstraße 6
24837 Schleswig

p: 04621. 963054

f: 04621. 963013

Wandmalereien im Kreuzgang des Domes
Wall paintings in the cloister at St. Petri's

Säulen für Germania

Pillars for Germania

Direkt an der Müllverbrennungsanlage Stuttgarts stehen fein aufgereiht 14 dorisch anmutende monumentale Säulen aus Naturstein. Die Kolossalsäulen stehen da wie bestellt und nicht abgeholt – und genau das ist auch ihre Geschichte.

Große Pläne hatten die Nazis für ihr Berlin, das fortan „Germania" heißen sollte. Gemeinsam mit seinem Lieblingsarchitekten Albert Speer plante Hitler massive Veränderungen im Berliner Stadtbild. Ein repräsentative Ost-West-Achse quer durch die Stadt war in den Planungen schon abgeschlossen und erste Bauarbeiten wurden kurz vor dem Krieg in Auftrag gegeben. Am westlichen Ende dieser Achse sollte ein Platz stehen (heute Theodor-Heuss-Platz), den Hitler seinem Freund Mussolini widmen wollte. Dazu musste ein ganz besonderes Denkmal her. Der Führer selbst lieferte die ersten Skizzen dazu, der Nazi-Bildhauer Arno Breker sollte die Skulptur liefern und Speer plante einen gigantischen Sockel, der aus zwei Säulenreihen bestand. Das Fundament wurde gegossen und die ersten Steinbestellungen ausgeschickt. Hitlers Lieblingsstein Travertin sollte verwendet werden. So bekam die Firma Lauster in Stuttgart den Auftrag, den sie auch sofort ausführte. Doch dann kam der Krieg, die Bauarbeiten für Germania wurden vorerst eingestellt und Lauster saß da mit seinen riesigen Säulen.

Doch der Lauster wäre kein richtiger Schwabe, wenn er nicht auch aus dieser Situation einen Vorteil für sich hätte herausholen können: Nach dem Krieg schwatzte er kurzerhand dem Staat die Säulen ab und stellte sie als Werbung vor sein Werk – übrigens eine beeindruckende Anlage, ganz in Naturstein mit vielen überraschenden Details.

Inzwischen ist die Firma Lauster schon lange nicht mehr an ihrem Standort in Stuttgart-Münster, die Werkhallen werden heute für Mülltrennung genutzt, die Säulen stehen aber noch da, ganz passend umgeben von Müllverwertungsfirmen.

Directly next to the waste incineration plant in Stuttgart, there are 14 monumental Doric-looking stone pillars, all neatly lined up in a long row. The gigantic columns look a bit as though they had been ordered by someone to be delivered, but then never picked up. In fact, this is exactly what happened.

The Nazis had big plans for their capital, Berlin. A new name was even planned for the city: Germania. Together with his favorite architect, Albert Speers, Hitler drew up massive alterations for the city's landscape. An East-West-Axis was to be built through the capital, and each part of this axis needed a representative plaza. The western square was to be dedicated to Mussolini, and a special monument was needed for the purpose. The Führer himself got to work on the sketches. Speer completed the planning, envisaging a giant pedestal made up of two rows of columns, and Sculptor Arno Brecker was decided on to create the sculpture. Construction started, and the foundation was quickly completed. The stonework, of course, had to be done using Hitler's very favorite stone, Travertine, which came out of Stuttgart. The stonemason company, Lauster, was commissioned to do the job and immediately got down to work, producing the columns in no time at all. Shortly after, however, the war began, and construction on the monument was discontinued. The pillars stayed in Stuttgart.

Lauster's founder, being a true Swabian (the Swabs are known for their diligence and frugality), decided to use the situation to his advantage. After the war, he took back his pillars, and put them in front of his plant to advertise his business. The plant, by the way, is also very interesting. The building is made completely out of stone and is full of lovely little details.

Today, the Lauster building is used as a garbage separation facility, but the pillars are still there – standing in front of a huge waste incineration plant. Fitting.

Die dorischen Säulen vor der Müllverbrennungsanlage
The Doric columns in front of the waste disposal plant

Lauster's Säulen
Lauster's Pillars
Neckartalstrasse 225
(an der Müllverbrennungs-anlage)
(close to the waste incineration plant)
70376 Stuttgart-Münster

·khalle der ehemaligen Steinmetz-Firma Lauster; heute wird hier der Müll getrennt
Workshop of the old Lauster stone works; where garbage is now separated

Steinrelief im Innern der Werkhalle
Stone relief inside the workshop

Der Koloss von Rügen

The Colossus of Rügen

Hinter dem schönsten Strand Rügens liegt die fünf Kilometer lange Ruine des „KDF (Kraft durch Freude) Seebads Rügen". 1936 konzipiert, sollte es als Massenschlafstätte für 20 000 „Volksgenossen" dienen. Robert Ley, der Leiter der Deutschen Arbeitsfront (DAF) und Gründer der KDF-Bewegung hatte es für den ersten organisierten Pauschalurlaub geplant: „Wenn es uns gelingt, ... jeden Deutschen jedes Jahr einmal zu überholen, dann behaupte ich, dass der Bruch der Leistungsfähigkeit des schaffenden Menschen nicht mehr bei 40 Jahren, sondern bei 70 Jahren liegen wird." Das Seebad sollte der Prototyp von fünf weiteren Erholungsbädern für den Deutschen werden. Das erste Wellenbad Europas, eine Anlegestelle für Dampfer und eine Logistik, wie sie noch nie zuvor gesehen worden war – die Pläne dieses Konzepts gewannen 1937 bei der Weltausstellung in Paris den Grand Prix.

Große Träume waren damit verknüpft, doch kam das Seebad nie über den Rohbau hinaus. Fast fertiggestellt, wurden dem Seebad sämtliche Geldhähne zugedreht – der Krieg hatte begonnen. Nach dem Krieg wurde es bis 1990 von der NVA genutzt, dann verließen auch die den Koloss. Heute steht es bis auf ein Museum und ein paar Künstlerniederlassungen leer. Vor ein paar Jahren versteckte sich ein jugendlicher Ausreißer in der Ruine. Jede Nacht schlief er in einem anderen Zimmer – die Polizei benötigte sechs Monate, um ihn zu finden.

Right behind Rügen's most beautiful beach, the five kilometer ruin of the "KDF Sea Resort Rügen" crumbles down along the Baltic Sea island (KDF was the third Reich's Strength Through Joy division, which aimed at systemizing the country's leisure and entertainment facilities). The resort was designed in 1936 and was supposed to have lodged up to 20,000 fascist holiday makers at any given time. The founder of the KDF and leader of the German Work Front (DAF), Dr. Robert Ley, intended for it to become the first organized packaged tour. According to Ley, "If we can manage to 'overhaul' every German once a year, we should be able to stretch the working power of each citizen up to 70 years, instead of only 40."

The sea resort was designated as a prototype, with five more to follow. There were plans to build the very first wave pool in Europe, plans for cruise ship docks, and for a logistical organization never before seen. These plans alone were so impressive that they won first prize in the Grand Prix at the World Exhibition in Paris in 1937.

Made of dreams, the resort never made it past the building's outer shell. The war started just as it was close to completion, and the money was used for other undertakings. After the war, parts of the building were used for a time by the East German army, but they too eventually lost interest, and the behemoth was simply abandoned. Apart from a museum, and a couple of artist's lofts, the five kilometer long building still stands empty. A few years ago, a runaway teen made use of the ruin, choosing a different room to sleep in every night. It took the police six months to find him.

Prora / Rügen
Objektstraße, Gebäude 1
18609 Prora

www.museum-prora.de/
prora.htm

Prora, soweit das Auge blickt
Prora, as far as the eye can see

Ehemaliges Kraftwerk, in dem der Raketenbrennstoff produziert wurde
The plant where rocket fuel was once produced

James Bond Insel
James Bond Island

Eine Insel unter einer Nebeldecke verschwinden lassen: klingt nach einem Trick aus 007. Nazis wendeten diesen Trick tatsächlich an, um ein 25 Quadratkilometer großes Gelände um das Fischerdorf Peenemünde auf der Insel Usedom vor Luftangriffen zu schützen. Denn hier lag seit 1936 das größte Forschungszentrum der Welt. Unter der Leitung von Wernher von Braun arbeiteten 15 000 Menschen, darunter auch KZ-Häftlinge, an der Entwicklung der Vergeltungswaffe V2: dem Vorläufer aller militärischer Langstreckenraketen und zivilen Weltraumträger. Am 3. Oktober 1942 gelang es der Gruppe um von Braun dann auch: Die erste Rakete der Menschheit wurde ins All geschossen. Seither wird Peenemünde von den einen als Wiege der Raumfahrt gelobt, von den anderen als Brutstätte von Massenvernichtungswaffen verschrien. Allein an der Entwicklung der Raketen starben mehr Menschen als durch ihren tatsächlichen Einsatz. Die Forscher und Ingenieure wurden von den Siegermächten rekrutiert und verhalfen ihnen zu einem schnellen Raketen- und Flugprogramm: Wernher von Braun stieg sogar zum Direktor der NASA auf.
Heute steht in Peenemünde noch das Kraftwerk, das den Treibstoff lieferte, als „Historisch Technisches Museum“

Hiding an island under a cloud of fog? Sounds like another 007 adventure; but during WWII, this was actually a reality for the 25 square km fishing village of Peenemünde, on the Baltic Sea island, Usedom. Here in 1936, the Nazis had built the worlds biggest research facility ever. Fifteen-thousand people (whose numbers were largely made up of concentration camp prisoners) worked to develop the famous V2-weapon under Wernher von Braun. It was the first of its kind and the forerunner of all military long distance weaponry and aerospace technology.
On November 3rd, 1942, the group around von Braun succeeded: They launched the very first rocket into outer space.
Peenemünde has since been caught in contention, some praising it as the cradle of space travel, others condemning it as the birthplace of weapons of mass destruction.
Interestingly, development of these rockets killed more people than the actual use of the weapons propelled by them. Surviving engineers from Peenemünde were recruited by the Allies, later helping to set up the aviation industries that would create so much pressure in international politics in the years after the war. Werner von Braun was even made director of NASA.

Modell vom Prüfstand VII
Model of Test Bed VII

umgebaut. Prüfstand VII, von dem aus die letzte Rakete 1945 gezündet wurde, lässt sich mit einem Bus erreichen. Zu Fuß wäre der Weg dahin noch heute lebensgefährlich: Im letzten Kriegsjahr wurde die Insel trotz Nebel massiv bombardiert, 20 Prozent Blindgänger stecken heute noch im Inselsand.

Today, the area of Peenemünde that was used for producing rocket fuel has been transformed into a technical museum, and the infamous Test Bed VII, from which the last rocket was launched in 1945, is open to visitors and can be reached by bus. Theoretically, it could also be reached by foot, but this is still too dangerous: Despite the fake fog implemented in 1944, Peenemünde was bombed more heavily than ever in this last year of the war. About one-fifth of the duds still remain, stuck somewhere in the island's white sand.

Detail einer V4 Rakete
Detail from a V4 Rocket

V4 Rakete
V4 Rocket

Im Innern des ehemaligen Kraftwerks
Inside the former production plant

Peenemünde
Im Kraftwerk
17449 Peenemünde

p: 038371. 5050

f: 038371. 505111

e: HTI@peenemuende.de

www.peenemuende.de/site/flash/ort.html

Öffnungszeiten:
April bis Oktober:
9.00 – 18.00 Uhr
November bis März:
10.00 – 16.00 Uhr
montags geschlossen,
Juni bis September auch montags geöffnet

Opening hours:
April to October:
9 am – 6 pm
November to March:
10 am – 4 pm
Mondays closed, except June to September

Atomarer Bierkeller
Atomic Beer-Cellar

Die Wiege der deutschen Atomforschung liegt nicht etwa in einem gut ausgestatteten Labor mit Sicherheitstrakt, sondern im Bierkeller einer Kneipe namens „Zum Schwanen", tief im Schwabenland, im Wallfahrtsort Haigerloch, wo sie keiner vermutet hätte. Und darum genau hier.

Zu Ende des Zweiten Weltkrieges, als Berlin derart unter Beschuss war, musste die Forschungsgruppe des Kaiser-Wilhelm-Institutes, zu der die Atomphysiker von Weizsäcker, Heisenberg, Hahn und Wirtz gehörten, an einen sicheren und geheimen Ort umziehen. In Haigerloch versteckt konnte zwar durch mit Neutronen beschossenes Uran eine selbsterhaltende Kettenreaktion in Gang gesetzt werden, jedoch fehlten die nötigen materiellen und technischen Möglichkeiten, um daraus atomwaffenfähiges Material herzustellen.

Am Ende des Krieges waren die amerikanischen Truppen die ersten, die in Haigerloch eintrafen und alles konfiszierten – zum Verdruss der anderen Besatzungsmächte. Die Wissenschaftler, die in Haigerloch tätig waren, wurden verhaftet und für US-amerikanische Projekte eingespannt.

Heute kann man den dunklen Keller, der nach der Demontage wieder als Bierkeller diente, besuchen. Die Stadt Haigerloch hat ihn zum Museum umgebaut, um die einzigartige Geschichte darzustellen. In ein paar Vitrinen stehen durch Uran grünlich gefärbte Laborgläser, den Mittelpunkt bildet der Apparat zur atomaren Kettenreaktion. Alles in allem etwas unspektakulär und gerade deshalb interessant.

The birthplace of German atomic research was not in some top-security high-Tec laboratory, but instead, in the beer-cellar of a traditional German Pub: Zum Schwanen (Swans Inn). The tavern can be found in the small town of Haigerloch, a famous place of pilgrimage in Southern Germany. Nice and low key – that was the plan.

In 1944, the war was still raging, and Berlin was under constant attack. The research group at the Emperor-Wilhelm-Institute decided that it was high time to move to a safer place. This group was made up of the famous researchers von Weizsäcker, Heisenberg, Wirtz, and Otto Hahn.

From their hiding place in Haigerloch, the scientists were able to initiate the first chain reaction created through the shelling of neutrons, but time ran out, preventing them from taking the next step in their creation of weapons of mass destruction.

At the end of the war, the Americans were the first to land in Haigerloch, and they took everything that they could find, including tools, knowledge, and even people. The researchers were taken into custody, and transferred to the U.S., where they immediately began working in American research facilities. The other allies were peeved.

After the Americans had thoroughly cleaned the basement out, it was put back into use as a beer-cellar. About ten years ago, the city of Haigerloch established a museum at the historical site. A couple of show-cases and a fake atomic reactor (complete with flashing blue lights) explain this important saga in the local history of Haigerloch. Nice and low key…

Modell vom Atomkeller
Model of the atomic-cellar

Eingang zum Bierkeller / Atomlabor
Entrance to the beer cellar/ atomic laboratory

Rekonstruktion des Versuchsreaktors
A reconstruction of the test reactor

Atomkeller-Museum (ehemalige Atomforschungs-stätte)
Atomic Cellar Museum (former atomic research lab)
Pfluggasse
(unter der Schlosskirche)
(below the Church of the Castle)
72394 Haigerloch

p: 07474. 69727

www.haigerloch.de

Öffnungszeiten:
Mo bis Sa
10.00 – 12.00 und
14.00 – 17.00 Uhr
So und Feiertag
10.00 – 17.00 Uhr
März, April, Oktober, November geschlossen.

Opening hours:
Tue to Sat from
10 am – noon and
2 pm – 5 pm
Sun from
10 am – 5 pm
March, April, Oktober, November closed.

Inhalt
Contents